CA ASIF **MASANI**

FROM ACCOUNTING TO FP&A

FROM NUMBER CRUNCHING TO
STRATEGIC THINKING

BEEJA
HOUSE

ISBN: 978-81-19682-09-6

Published by: Beeja House

Printed By: Repro India Pvt. Ltd.

First Printing Edition 2024

Author Website: www.asifmasani.com

I Want To Dedicate this book,

To my parents, whose unwavering support and encouragement have been the foundation of my journey.

To my brother Nadeem, for his constant inspiration and belief in my dreams.

To my wife CA Kajal, for her endless patience, love, and understanding, which made this dream a reality.

This book is for you.

Disclaimer

The concepts and practices described in this book are broadly applicable to various roles within finance department. While the term "Financial Planning and Analysis (FP&A)" is used throughout, it is important to note that the function and responsibilities of FP&A may not be labelled as such in every organization.

Different companies may use alternative titles to refer to similar finance roles and functions. The concepts shared in this book are applicable to all business finance roles (business facing finance roles).

While every effort has been made to ensure the accuracy of the information contained in this book, the author and publisher accept no responsibility for any errors or omissions. The information provided is for educational purposes and should be tailored to meet the unique needs and standards of your professional environment.

Foreword

I am delighted to write the foreword for "From Accounting to FP&A" by Asif Masani. Over the past two years, I have had the privilege of working closely with Asif, witnessing his dedication and expertise in Financial Planning and Analysis (FP&A). His work has profoundly impacted many professionals, including myself.

People often ask us how we got into FP&A training and coaching. The story began in 2022 when Asif, after writing numerous posts and articles on LinkedIn, compiled enough material to publish his first book, "All About FP&A." The book's success led to an overwhelming number of requests for FP&A training. Around the same time, I had been training and coaching thousands of finance professionals through my online program, "FP&A Foundations," which received excellent reviews and feedback.

Seeing the opportunity to combine our forces and expertise, we decided to work together. With over two decades of FP&A experience across five different industries, we set a common mission: To help 1 million finance professionals master FP&A skills. In October 2022, we launched our inaugural FP&A Masterclass batch with 25 students, aiming to develop a curriculum that reflected the training we wished we had at the beginning of our FP&A careers and what we would teach our new team members today.

Two years and over a dozen batches later, our curriculum has evolved significantly based on feedback from over 350 participants. Along the way, we've received hundreds of testimonials and success stories, highlighting the positive impact of our training programs.

Asif's journey is marked by his commitment to excellence and his deep understanding of the finance landscape. His book, "From Accounting to FP&A," bridges the gap between traditional accounting roles and the dynamic world of FP&A. It offers practical advice, strategic insights, and real-world examples, making complex financial concepts accessible to all.

Working with Asif has been an enriching experience. His passion for mentoring and his ability to inspire those around him have left an indelible mark on my professional journey. I am confident that this book will be a valuable resource for anyone looking to succeed in FP&A.

I highly recommend "From Accounting to FP&A" and believe it will empower you to reach new heights in your career.

Dhawal Parvatikar
Co-Founder & Lead Faculty,
FP&A Professionals Institute (FPI)

Endorsements and Praises for "From Accounting to FP&A"

"An extremely well-written guide covering each step-in transitioning into and succeeding in FP&A and business finance roles. Asif carries great expertise in enabling the finance community in FP&A and business finance. Through this very well-written book, he provides excellent guidance to finance professionals who are exploring a career shift into these roles that are the future of the finance function. I strongly recommend it."

R. Ravikumar
Ex-CFO, IBM India and author of THE CFO LENS

***

"Asif Masani's latest book "From Accounting to FP&A" is an indispensable guide for accoutring and business professionals looking to transition their career from accounting to FP&A. The 12 chapters in the book provides a comprehensive roadmap, blending practical insights with strategic frameworks. Throughout the book, Asif demystifies complex financial concepts and processes, making them accessible to readers with diverse backgrounds. One of the standout features of this book is its real-world applicability.

Through detailed case studies and practical examples, readers can see the direct impact of FP&A strategies on business decision-making and performance. Whether you're an experienced accountant seeking to broaden your skill set or a newcomer eager to enter the world of FP&A, this book offers clear, actionable, and practical guidance to navigate the shift smoothly. I highly recommend "From Accounting to FP&A" and I strongly believe this book will empower you to take your career to the next level."

Dr. Prashanth Southekal
Founder and Managing Principal at DBP Institute, Author of Data for Business *Performance, Analytics Best Practices and Data Quality*

***

"Asif has complete command over how to make FP&A's role within an organization enormously impactful. His book, From Accounting to FP&A, highlights his leadership in this area. The detailed 'A Day in Life' examples and the 'First 90 Days in the Role' leave no doubt about his deep expertise and his ability to communicate it through the written word. He emphasizes the growing mandate CFOs and other business leaders are demanding of their FP&A teams and From Accounting to FP&A is the 'how to' book for FP&A leaders to satisfy that demand."

Steve Rosvold
Founder at CFO.University

***

"It takes one to know one and Asif is an FP&A professional at heart who has experienced what it takes to move from Audit and Accounting into FP&A first hand. He uses his experience to coach and mentor accountants on how to make the move themselves and now he has elegantly captured this in his latest book

"From Accounting to FP&A". This is the most common career path in the finance function and Asif's mission to help 1 million finance and accounting professionals master FP&A gets my full endorsement!"

Anders Liu-Lindberg

Partner and Co-founder at Business Partnering Institute

Author of "Create value as a Finance Business Partner".

***

"Transitioning from Accounting to FP&A is a common career path and one people ask me about regularly and that is why this book is sorely needed. Asif is a global expert in this area and has helped many people make the transition from accounting to FP&A and this book will serve as a great resource for those looking for some help in deciding if FP&A is right for them and then making the transition to FP&A."

Paul Barnhurst, Founder The FP&A Guy
Podcast Host at FP&A Tomorrow, Financial Modeler's Corner and Co-host at Future Finance Podcast.

***

"From Accounting to FP&A: From Number Crunching to Strategic Thinking" by CA Asif Masani is an invaluable resource for anyone seeking to transition into or advance within the FP&A field. The book offers structured guidance and actionable insights, making it essential for finance professionals at various stages of their careers.

Masani combines theoretical knowledge with practical experience, distilling wisdom from over 20 expert interviews. The book provides a comprehensive framework, building the reader's understanding from basic FP&A roles and responsibilities to advanced strategies for excelling in these positions.

This book serves as a comprehensive manual that equips finance professionals with the necessary tools and insights to excel in the FP&A domain. Whether you are a beginner exploring career options, a new FP&A professional seeking to bridge knowledge gaps, or a mid-career professional transitioning from accounting to FP&A, this book provides a clear, actionable path to success. Highly recommended for its depth, clarity, and practical relevance."

Saleem Sufi, Dean & Director, MECA CFO Academy (CFOAcademy.org)
Author of "YOUR PATH TO C-SUITE: A Career Guide for Hungry and Foolish"

***

Acknowledgements

The following FP&A Leaders have contributed to the book (in no particular order):

Abhinav Aggarwal, Akshay Phadke, Dhawal Parvatikar, Swati Bagri, Brett Hampson, Jason Hershman, Mohamed ElRouby, Rohit Daiya, Arpit Chandak, Shreya Shanbhag, Vivek Sharma, Ron Monteiro, Gaurav Malik, George Katsimihas, Ali Hassan, Ammar Bin Saqib and Jun Nichole Villanueva.

I thank everyone for taking time out of their busy schedules and sharing their input, experiences, and guidance that have influenced this book's content. I am most grateful to them for sharing their time, expertise and knowledge.

I would also like to extend my heartfelt thanks to Geetika Saigal (Beeja Education) for her unwavering support and dedication throughout the publishing process. I am also grateful to the project manager, Saakshi Kaushal and Shristy Thawait who helped with the cover and graphics for the book on Beeja's team. And to CA Sweta Jhalani who managed the entire book project, helping me every step of the way.

Note From The Author

I frequently receive emails and LinkedIn messages from people who have read my first book "All About FP&A" or participated in one of our live workshops "FP&A Masterclass" or taken our self-paced course "FP&A Launchpad".

There are notes of encouragement, support for the work we're doing, and plenty of questions and requests. I enjoy hearing success stories, such as successful job interviews, promotions, and stories about influencing business decisions or making a positive impact on an organisation's bottom line.

The most inspiring are those of personal growth and recognition. The most common situation is when a reader uses "All About FP&A" principles during an interview, and it helps them get a new job with better pay and position. In many cases, a new FP&A role with pay in multiples of 2X or more from the previous role.

This success is thanks to people from different industries, functions, and roles dedicating time to improving their FP&A skills. I also hear regularly from people who want more.

After reading the book "All About FP&A", they realise the value of FP&A skills. However, they struggle with transitioning from their current roles, which are mainly in accounting, audit, tax, or compliance.

They have additional questions or feel they are facing nuanced situations that are keeping them from taking the leap. It's clear to me that people crave more guidance to help successfully navigate this challenging transition phase. This book addresses this transition challenge for accountants, auditors, and non-finance professionals.

By sharing invaluable insights not just from my experience but the collective wisdom I have gathered from 20+ expert interviews who have successfully made the transition. This book will boost your confidence and add more credibility as you transition from accounting/audit/controller positions to Financial Planning and Analysis (FP&A) roles.

CA Asif Masani
Co-Founder FP&A Professionals Institute (FPI)

Contents

Section 1

Introduction And FP&A Mindset

Chapter 1

The Evolving Role Of Finance: From Accounting To Strategy

At first, finance mainly looked back at past financial performance. But as business got more data and improved technology, there was a shift.

Businesses realised financial information shouldn't just look back; it should help plan the future. This is where FP&A came in, using past data to forecast future trends and help guide business decisions. New tools and technology have made it possible to get deeper insights from financial and operational data.

Towards Business Partnering

Next, FP&A started to become a business partner, not just analysing data but also working closely with different parts of the business to shape strategies. This change was helped by advances in technology like automation, cloud computing and AI making it easier to analyse data and offer strategic advice. As businesses needed to move faster, having a team focused on strategic financial planning became crucial.

Current State: The Strategic FP&A

Now, FP&A is vital for setting business strategy.

Its not just about controlling costs but also finding opportunities for growth and advising on big decisions. FP&A professionals now need a mix of finance skills, strategic thinking, and the ability to communicate complex information clearly.

Moving forward, FP&A will become even more strategic.

New technologies will provide more tools for analysis and forecasting, helping businesses make even better decisions.

FP&A Professionals will have to keep up with these technologies and learn how to filter through more and more data. We will also need to continue developing our strategic skills to help shape business strategy.

For those in FP&A, this evolution offers a chance to play a crucial role in our company's success and build a dynamic career.

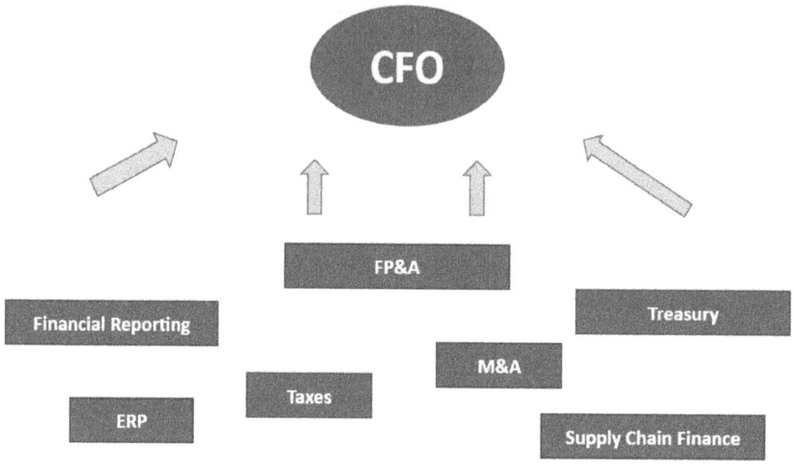

Different Roles Reporting to the CFO

If you look at a typical Chief Finance Officers (CFO's) office. There are multiple roles or functions reporting to the CFO.

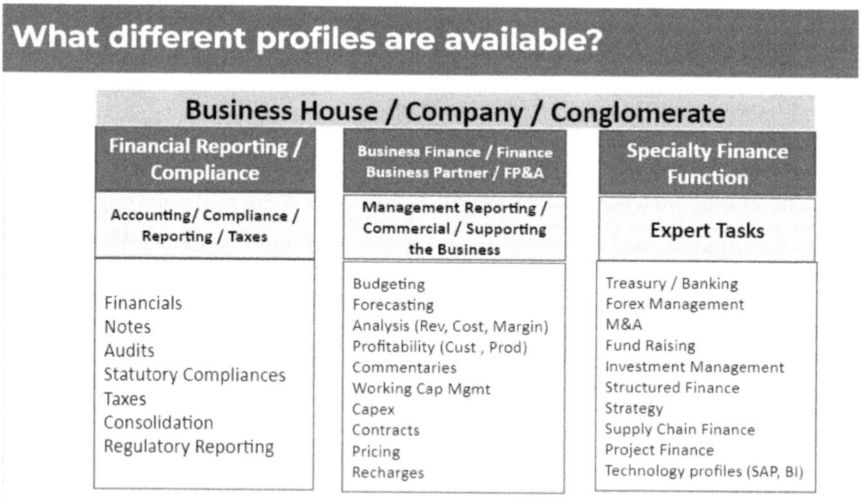

We can classify these roles into three main buckets:

1. Financial Reporting & Compliance.
2. Decision Support, and
3. Specialty or Expert Tasks.

1. Financial Reporting & Compliance

Financial Reporting & Compliance roles are fundamental to the integrity and transparency of any organisation. They are the bedrock of any finance department.

Professionals in this category are responsible for the accurate representation of a company's financial health through financial statements, ensuring compliance with statutory requirements, and managing internal and external audits.

These roles are essential for maintaining the trust of investors, regulators, and other stakeholders by ensuring the company's financial practices are in line with legal and regulatory standards.

The role of Financial Reporting is not just about looking back at what has happened; it's also about ensuring the company is able to move forward compliantly. From the preparation of balance sheets, income statements, and cash flow statements to the intricate details of notes to accounts, these functions form the backbone of financial transparency. Compliance roles extend this further by navigating the complex web of tax filings, including GST (indirect taxes in India) and corporate taxes, thereby safeguarding the company against financial and legal risks.

2. Decision Support

As businesses evolve, the need for strategic financial insight becomes important. This is where Decision Support roles come into play, acting as a strategic partner to the business.

This category includes functions like budgeting, forecasting, financial analysis, and management reporting. Professionals in this bucket work closely with senior management, providing the insights necessary for informed decision-making.

They analyse data, predict future trends, and offer recommendations to optimize financial performance and achieve strategic goals.

The focus here is on supporting business decisions with financial and business acumen.

Whether it's conducting profitability analysis, managing working capital, or setting pricing strategies, Decision Support roles ensure that every business decision is grounded in solid financial rationale.

This proactive approach enables companies to stay ahead in the competitive market, adapt to changes swiftly, and capitalize on new opportunities.

3. Specialty or Expert Tasks

The finance function also includes roles that require specialized knowledge and expertise. Examples of these include areas like forex management, hedging, fundraising, investment management, and supply chain finance.

Professionals in this bucket tackle complex financial challenges, manage risks, and drive innovation within their domain.

This category extends beyond traditional finance roles, diving into areas that require a deep understanding of both finance principles and the specific operational contexts of a business.

Here's a detailed exploration of this third bucket:

Treasury

The Treasury team manages banking relations and ensures the company has sufficient working capital.

Forex Management and Hedging

In an increasingly globalised economy, companies are more exposed to currency fluctuations than ever before. Forex management and hedging involve protecting the company from unfavourable shifts in exchange rates. Specialists in this area use financial instruments to hedge against risks, ensuring that the company's international transactions do not lead to unexpected losses.

Fundraising and Investment Management

Raising capital and managing investments are critical for sustaining growth and building the company's future. This includes identifying and securing funding sources, whether through equity, debt, or other financial instruments.

Investment management focuses on making strategic decisions about how to allocate the company's capital to maximize returns while managing risk.

Supply Chain Finance

This speciality area aims to improve financial efficiency across the supply chain. By optimising payment terms and leveraging financial solutions, companies can enhance their working capital, reduce costs, and strengthen relationships with suppliers. Supply chain finance requires a blend of finance expertise and deep knowledge of supply chain operations.

Project Finance

Project finance is crucial for funding large-scale projects, often in industries like infrastructure, energy, and construction. This role involves structuring financing arrangements that rely on the future cash flows generated by the project for repayment. Professionals in this field assess the feasibility of projects, manage financial risks, and arrange the necessary funding.

Technology and Functional Consulting

As businesses increasingly rely on technology to drive efficiency and innovation, the role of finance professionals with technology expertise grows in importance. Functional consultants act as a bridge between finance and IT, helping to design and implement finance systems, ERP solutions, and business intelligence tools. They must understand the technological needs of the finance function and ensure that tech solutions align with business goals.

The third bucket of speciality finance roles focuses on expert tasks, underscores the breadth and depth of finance as a discipline.

The three broad buckets highlight the dynamic nature of finance roles in addressing complex, specialised challenges that businesses face today.

These roles demand a high level of expertise, strategic thinking, and often, an understanding of specific industries or technological solutions. As businesses continue to navigate a complex global environment.

The demand for professionals skilled in each of these finance roles is set to grow, reflecting the critical role they play in steering companies toward sustainable growth and resilience.

Understanding the FP&A role

Think of FP&A as the core team that links what's happening day-to-day in a business with the big-picture plans of company leaders. It's this team's job to balance current activities with future goals. This makes FP&A a key player in any company's success.

Key Activities in FP&A

At its core, FP&A can be dissected into two main types of activities:

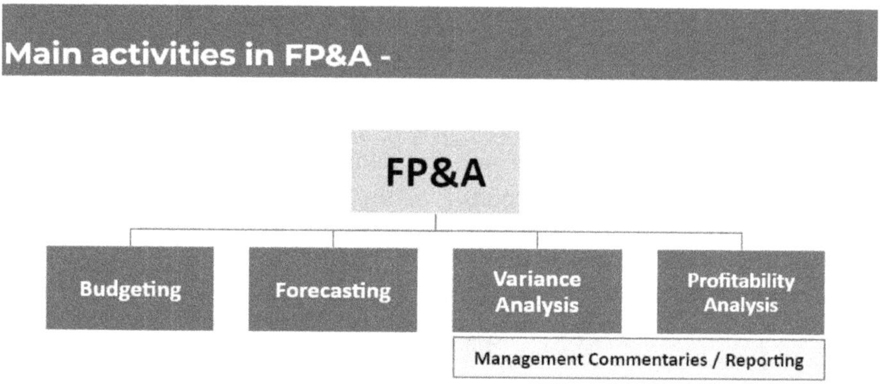

1. Financial Planning and
2. Financial Analysis.

Together, they form the backbone of a company's financial strategy, enabling it to navigate through the complexities of the market with agility and precision.

Financial Planning: Charting the Course

"Financial Planning is like preparing a ship to sail towards its goal."

It's about carefully making business plans and predicting future finances to match the company's big plans. This task looks ahead and requires a good grasp of how the business works, what the market looks like, and what obstacles might pop up.

The essence of financial planning lies in its collaborative nature.

FP&A professionals work closely with various business units—be it sales, marketing, HR, or operations—to gather insights and understand their financial needs and goals. This collaboration ensures that the financial plan not only captures the company's vision but is also deeply rooted in operational realities.

A well-structured financial plan serves as a guiding light for the organisation, providing a clear framework within which it can operate and make strategic decisions. It outlines the resources required for different initiatives. And anticipates financial needs, and sets benchmarks against which performance can be measured.

Financial Analysis: Navigating the Terrain

"If financial planning sets the course, then Financial Analysis is the compass that helps navigate the terrain."

It's an ongoing process that involves scrutinising the company's financial health and operational performance. This is where the rubber meets the road—FP&A professionals dive into variance analysis, comparing actual results against the budget, forecast, and previous periods' performance.

This analysis shows where the company stands in terms of achieving its financial goals. It helps identify trends, pinpoints discrepancies, and uncovers underlying root causes of variances. This continuous monitoring and evaluation enable businesses to respond quickly to changes, make informed decisions, and steer the company in the right direction.

Moreover, financial analysis isn't just about looking at the numbers; it's about interpreting them in a way that provides actionable insights. Whether it's making a pricing decision, adjusting revenue strategies, or refining operational processes, the analysis carried out by FP&A professionals plays a critical role in guiding these decisions.

Relationship of Planning and Analysis

"Financial Planning and Financial Analysis are not standalone processes"

They are inherently interconnected. The cycle of planning, executing, analysing, and revising is a dynamic and ongoing process. A well-formulated financial plan sets the stage, but it's the continuous analysis that ensures the plan remains relevant and effective.

This relationship between planning and analysis ensures that the organisation remains agile, able to adapt its strategy based on real-time insights and emerging trends.

FP&A represents the coming together of strategic foresight and operational insight.

By focussing on both Financial Planning and Financial Analysis. FP&A translates strategic objectives into actionable plans and ensures those plans yield the desired outcomes.

FP&A not only helps companies chart their course with confidence but also equips them with the tools to navigate the journey effectively. This dual focus on planning for the future while analysing the present is what makes FP&A an indispensable part of modern business strategy.

The Vital Bridge of FP&A

On one side, there are the business teams like sales, marketing, HR, and operations—these are the folks getting things done everyday, each with their own tasks and challenges.

Figure 1- Picture FP&A as bridge

On the other side, you have the top bosses like CEOs and CFOs, looking ahead and deciding where the company should head next.

FP&A stands in the middle, making sure both sides are connected and working together smoothly.

Just as the bridge helps commute between two sides. FP&A teams actively help the two sides communicate.

They turn the day-to-day data into big-picture insights, ensuring leaders make informed, data-backed decisions that truly reflect what's happening in the business.

Let's dive into some examples that highlight how FP&A acts as a bridge, specifically during the processes of budgeting, forecasting, and management reporting:

1. Budgeting Process:

In the budgeting process, FP&A teams start by engaging with various business units, such as sales, marketing, and operations.

They gather information about each team's financial needs and goals for the upcoming period. This process isn't just about collecting numbers. It involves understanding the strategic initiatives each department plans to undertake. And the resources they'll need, and the challenges they anticipate.

Once the FP&A team has gathered all this information. They compile it into a comprehensive budget. This draft budget is then reviewed in collaboration with the business units to ensure it accurately reflects their plans and resources required.

Let's say for example.

At a mid-sized tech company, the FP&A team starts the annual budgeting process by scheduling meetings with the heads of various departments, including sales, marketing, and operations. During these sessions, they don't just collect budget numbers but dive deep into the strategic initiatives each department intends to pursue in the coming year.

For instance, the marketing department plans to launch a new product that will require a significant advertising budget and additional staff. The operations team anticipates the need for upgraded software to handle increased production volume. Understanding these nuances allows the FP&A team to craft a budget that supports these strategic goals.

The FP&A team fine-tunes the budget based on feedback, ensuring it aligns with the company's overall strategic goals.

The final step involves presenting this consolidated budget to senior management for approval.

Here, FP&A acts as the bridge by translating the operational needs and plans of the business units into a financial document that senior management can review, understand, and approve.

This ensures that the company's strategic direction and resource allocation harmonise with the day-to-day operational plans and capabilities.

2. Management Reporting

During the management reporting process, FP&A collects and analyses data from various sources within the company. This includes sales figures, marketing expenses, operational costs, and more. They synthesise this data into actionable insights, highlighting trends, variances from the budget, and areas requiring attention.

These insights are not just numbers on a page. They tell the story of how the company is performing against its goals and what factors are influencing that performance. The FP&A team presents these findings in management reports to senior executives, providing them with a clear, concise, and comprehensive view of the company's financial health and operational performance.

In this way, FP&A ensures that senior management's decisions are informed by up-to-date, accurate, and relevant data.

By interpreting the operational data and presenting it in a strategic context, FP&A helps bridge the gap between day-to-day activities and long-term strategic planning, allowing leaders to make informed decisions that drive the company forward.

3. Forecasting Process

The forecasting process typically starts mid-year or quarterly, depending on the company's needs, distinct from the annual budgeting cycle.

During the forecasting process, the FP&A team again engages closely with various business units to understand their current activities, upcoming initiatives, and any expected changes in their operational environment. This engagement is crucial because it provides the FP&A team with the operational insights needed to make accurate forecasts.

The FP&A team starts by collecting detailed information from the sales, marketing, HR, and operations teams. They discuss potential market changes, sales trends, marketing campaigns, staffing needs, and operational challenges. This step is about understanding not just the "what" but the "why" behind each team's expectations for the future.

With this information, FP&A develops a financial forecast that projects future revenues, expenses, cash flow, and other key financial metrics over the upcoming period. This forecast is based on the combination of historical data and the new insights gathered from each business unit, adjusted for expected changes in the business environment.

Before finalising the forecast, the FP&A team reviews their initial projections with the business units to ensure they accurately reflect the operational plans and expectations. This iterative process may involve several rounds of adjustment to align the forecast with the most current and comprehensive understanding of the company's operational outlook.

The completed forecast is then presented to senior management. **In this crucial step, FP&A acts as a bridge by translating the detailed operational insights and expectations into a strategic financial outlook.** This enables senior leaders to understand the financial implications of the company's operational plans, assess risks and opportunities, and make informed strategic decisions.

Through forecasting, FP&A facilitates a continuous flow of information and insights between the operational heart of the business and its strategic head.

This ongoing dialogue ensures that the company's financial strategy is always grounded in operational reality and that operational plans are always informed by financial insight.

In essence, FP&A helps the company move forward with a clear view: paying attention to day-to-day operations while also planning for the future.

As we delve deeper, In Chapter 2 let's explore what motivates professionals to make the significant shift from accounting and audit roles into FP&A.

Chapter 2

Motivations For Moving To FP&A

Importance of transitioning from Accounting to FP&A

Transitioning from accounting and audit roles to FP&A represents a significant career shift that can unlock plenty of opportunities.

While accounting and audit are fundamental to the financial health and compliance of any organisation, FP&A offers a broader perspective, focusing on the future financial direction of the company.

Motivations for moving into FP&A

"In my opinion, FP&A opens many opportunities within finance and accounting. For young professionals starting out, I always recommend FP&A because you'll gain a deep understanding of the business, which covers roles like project management, data analysis, and management control, in addition to basic daily accounting operations. In FP&A, you'll soon realise what you specifically want to do in the future. For me, it was about setting up processes and standards, ensuring accurate numbers for decision-making, which steered me towards a financial controller role."

- *Jun Nichole*

Embarking on the journey from audit and accounting to FP&A is undeniably challenging.

There will be moments of doubt, steep learning curves, and instances where the path ahead seems obscured.

In these times, it's important to anchor yourself to your core motivations for making this transition.

Whether it's the appeal of playing a strategic role in shaping the future of your company, the personal and professional growth that comes from mastering a broader skill set, the fulfilment derived from impacting business outcomes directly, the collaborative nature of working across functions, or the dynamism of the FP&A role, remembering what drew you to this path can provide the strength to persevere.

So, when the journey feels particularly challenging, ask yourself: which of these motivations resonates most with you?

Identifying your primary motivator can rekindle your passion and drive, guiding you through the hurdles to achieve your career aspirations in FP&A.

Let's explore the typical motivations behind this career shift, and why many choose to navigate from the structured world of audit and accounting to the dynamic field of FP&A.

1. **Seeking a Strategic Role**

Audit and accounting play a vital role in ensuring financial accuracy and regulatory compliance, providing a solid foundation for any business's financial health. Professionals in these fields excel in detail-oriented tasks that require a deep understanding of financial standards and principles.

However, for many, the desire to influence future outcomes and participate in proactive decision-making sparks an interest in FP&A. One of the most significant benefits of moving into FP&A is the opportunity to directly impact business strategy.

FP&A plays a key role in steering the company towards its goals by providing insights that inform business decisions.

They work closely with senior management, offering analyses and financial models that predict future financial performance and highlight potential risks and opportunities.

This involvement allows FP&A professionals to see the direct results of their work, as they participate in planning and decision-making processes that shape the company's future.

FP&A offers a platform to apply financial expertise in a manner that directly influences corporate strategy and future growth. ***This provides a compelling reason for professionals to transition, as it allows them to not only report on what has happened but also shape what could happen.***

2. Broadening Skill Sets

"Transitioning between different roles in finance, such as from audit to FP&A or from FP&A to M&A, is about leveraging transferable skills. My own journey from investment banking to an MBA in the USA was driven by a desire to gain a global perspective and develop leadership skills by interacting with a diverse group of students. This educational experience broadened my career opportunities both within and outside of finance." – Akshay Phadke

Accounting and audit roles are essential for maintaining financial integrity by focusing on historical data to ensure accuracy and compliance with financial regulations. Professionals in these areas are experts in reporting, compliance, auditing, and ensuring that financial statements accurately reflect past business activities.

While these functions are crucial, they often limit professionals to a reactive position, dealing with the aftermath of financial decisions rather than participating in the decision-making process.

FP&A, on the other hand, is forward-looking.

It involves budgeting, forecasting, and analysing financial data to guide business decisions.

Transitioning to FP&A allows professionals to use their financial acumen to influence the future direction of the business, moving from recording and reporting financial history to shaping financial futures.

The move to FP&A demands and fosters a broader skill set. At the same time, the foundation of strong financial knowledge is vital. FP&A roles require additional competencies such as advanced analytical skills, business acumen, and the ability to synthesise and communicate complex information to influence decisions.

Professionals motivated by personal growth see FP&A as an opportunity to enhance their abilities beyond the technicalities of accounting and audit. ***They are drawn to the challenge of developing new skills, such as financial modelling, strategic analysis, and data-driven storytelling, which are critical in a role that supports business leaders in making informed decisions.***

3. Impacting Business Outcomes

"Career growth in FP&A is primarily analytical and typically doesn't revert back to compliance roles like preparing financial statements. People in FP&A might start as analysts and can evolve into roles that involve more business finance responsibilities. For instance, they could help set up a new business unit from scratch, dealing with elements like pricing and management reports. Over time, one can expect to handle a variety of commercial tasks and potentially rise to a CFO position, where you transition from an individual contributor to a leadership role, continually learning and training others"

- ***Dhawal Parvatikar***

Audit and accounting roles ensure an organization's financial health and compliance, supporting the strategic direction through meticulous oversight and control.

In contrast, FP&A professionals are front and centre in driving business performance and outcomes. They analyse trends, forecast future performance, and provide insights that guide budgeting, investments, and other business decisions.

This potential to impact business outcomes directly is a significant draw for those looking to make a tangible difference within their organisation. The ability to see the results of one's work reflected in the company's strategic direction and financial success is highly rewarding.

4. Seeking Cross-functional Collaboration

FP&A professional's work at the intersection of finance and operations, collaborating with various departments to gather information and provide financial insights.

This cross-functional interaction is different from the siloed nature of traditional accounting and audit roles. FP&A offers professionals a comprehensive view of the organisation.

Through regular interaction with different business units, FP&A professionals develop a deeper understanding of the company's operations, priorities, and challenges.

This holistic perspective is crucial for effective financial planning and analysis, as it enables FP&A to provide more relevant and impactful advice.

Professionals motivated by the desire for a more integrated role within the company find FP&A appealing for the opportunity it provides to understand and contribute to the business holistically. This cross-functional collaboration enriches their understanding of the business, enhances their ability to provide meaningful insights, and positions them as business partners across the organisation.

5. Desire for a Dynamic Work Environment

"It's important to recognise that career progression in FP&A isn't always a linear path. You might start in one role and as you discover what you enjoy, you can pivot to different areas within finance and accounting, just like several of my teammates who have moved into roles like project management and business operations."

– *Asif Masani*

Audit and accounting are integral to any business, offering stability and reliability through established cycles of reporting and compliance activities. For some, the appeal of FP&A lies in its dynamic nature.

FP&A role thrives on professionals requiring adapting quickly to new information, market trends, and business needs.

The fast-paced environment, coupled with the challenge of forecasting and planning in uncertain conditions, attracts those looking for a career that keeps them on their toes. ***The satisfaction of contributing to business decisions in real time is a powerful motivator.***

The transition from audit and accounting to FP&A can be fuelled by a diverse range of motivations. From the desire to play a more strategic role and impact business outcomes to the pursuit of personal growth through skill development and cross-functional collaboration, the move is attractive for many reasons.

Additionally, FP&A offers a refreshing change for those seeking to escape the predictability of traditional finance roles. As the business world continues to evolve, the role of FP&A becomes increasingly critical, offering a rewarding career path for those looking to make a significant impact within their organisations.

Growth opportunities in the FP&A field

FP&A stands at the convergence of finance, strategy, and decision-making, offering a dynamic and influential career path for professionals in the finance sector.

With businesses increasingly prioritising financial planning to navigate the complexities of global markets, the demand for skilled FP&A professionals has surged.

Let's look at some of the potential growth opportunities in FP&A:

Traditionally viewed as budget managers and number crunchers, FP&A professionals today are recognised as partners in the business. They are involved in shaping the company's future through insightful analysis, forecasting, and planning. This has opened up new dimensions of growth and development.

1. **Strategic Influence and Leadership**

One of the most compelling growth opportunities in FP&A is the potential for strategic influence. FP&A work closely with senior management, providing the insights necessary to inform business decisions and guide the company's direction. This close collaboration with decision-makers not only elevates the role of FP&A within the company but also positions FP&A professionals as candidates for leadership roles.

As they gain experience, they can climb to positions like Chief Financial Officer (CFO), where they can shape the company's financial and operational strategy at the highest level.

2. **Specialisation and Niche Expertise**

FP&A offers diverse pathways for specialisation. This allows professionals to deepen their expertise in specific industries, functions, or types of analysis.

For instance, one might specialize in financial modelling or data storytelling, or sector-specific financial analysis (such as technology, healthcare, or manufacturing). Developing niche expertise not only enhances an individual's value to their current organisation but also increases their marketability, opening doors to specialized roles across industries.

3. Network Building

FP&A's inherently collaborative nature offers unique opportunities for professionals to build extensive internal networks. By working closely with various departments—such as sales, marketing, operations, and HR—FP&A professionals gain a comprehensive understanding of the business. This broad exposure not only enriches their analytical skills but also positions them as connectors within the company, fostering relationships that can drive their careers forward through diverse opportunities and internal mobility.

4. Global Opportunities and Mobility

As businesses expand globally, the demand for FP&A professionals who can navigate international finance complexities grows.

This globalisation offers FP&A professionals opportunities to work in different markets, understand diverse business environments, and tackle unique financial challenges. ***The ability to work across borders enhances their global financial acumen, making them valuable assets to multinational corporations and opening international career pathways.***

5. Continuous Learning and Professional Development

Driven by technological advancements, regulatory changes, and market fluctuations—requires FP&A professionals to be lifelong learners. These educational pursuits not only broaden their skill set but also enhance their career advancement prospects.

6. Technology and Innovation

With data analytics, artificial intelligence (AI), and machine learning playing increasingly critical roles. FP&A professionals with a knack for technology can lead initiatives to implement and leverage new financial tools and platforms, driving efficiency and insights. This intersection of finance and technology offers a fertile ground for innovation, allowing FP&A professionals to pioneer new analytical methodologies and decision-making frameworks.

A career in FP&A is ripe with opportunities for growth, development, and influence.

Whether through leadership roles, specialisation, cross-functional collaboration, global mobility, continuous learning, or technological innovation, FP&A professionals have numerous paths to elevate their careers.

For those looking to make a meaningful impact within their organisations and beyond, FP&A offers a challenging yet rewarding career trajectory, marked by constant evolution and the potential to shape the future of business.

Navigating the Transition

Making the transition from accounting and audit to FP&A can be challenging, but it is also rewarding. It requires a willingness to move beyond the comfort zone of established procedures and standards, embracing a more dynamic and uncertain world where financial data is used to predict and shape the future.

It offers the chance to move from a primarily retrospective focus to a role that actively shapes the future trajectory of an organisation. By embracing this shift, professionals can broaden their impact, enhance their skills, and play a pivotal role in driving their company's business decisions.

As the businesses continue to evolve, the demand for skilled FP&A professionals is set to rise, making this transition not just valuable, but essential for those looking to advance their careers in finance.

Understanding the motivations is just the beginning. Next, in Chapter 3 we'll uncover the 12 essential mindset shifts required to excel in FP&A.

Chapter 3

The FP&A Mindset Shift

This chapter talks about why accountants should start thinking more like FP&A professionals.

Traditionally, accountants focus a lot on past numbers and making sure everything adds up correctly. In FP&A you look ahead and use numbers to help make decisions about the future of the business.

While you move from the traditional accounting and compliance role to FP&A roles. You are now more involved in shaping where the company is going, not just keeping track of where it's been.

In this chapter let's explore the 12 necessary mindset shifts along with what benefits it brings to you.

Here are the top 12 mindset Shifts from Accounting to FP&A

1. From Past to Future
2. From Number Crunching to Strategic Thinking
3. From Detailed Oriented to Big Picture Thinking
4. Risk Aversion to Comfort with Ambiguity
5. Silos to Cross-functional Collaboration
6. From Data to Insights
7. From Accounting Jargon to Simple Language
8. From Building Processes to Building Relationships
9. From Numbers to Storytelling
10. From Email to Face-to-Face Communication
11. From Challenging to Coaching
12. From Telling to Influencing

1. From Past to Future

Accountants typically focus on recording and reporting past financial activities. They ensure everything is accurate and meets regulations.

On the other hand, FP&A professionals look to the future. They use past data to build models and predict what might happen next. This helps companies plan and make decisions.

This proactive approach is preparing for the future rather than just reviewing the past.

Example: *Amcor Inc. usually spends a lot on marketing without really checking if it's worth it.*

An accountant's job is to make sure the costs from these past marketing efforts are recorded correctly according to the rules.

But someone working in FP&A wouldn't stop there.

They'd look at how much money these marketing efforts made in return, use that data to guess how future spending might help sales, and suggest changes to the budget.

For instance, they might recommend spending more in areas where it's really paying off and cutting spending where it's not. This approach helps the company make better choices for future growth and financial health.

2. From Number Crunching to Strategic Thinking

Accountants focus mainly on making sure that the financial records are correct. They follow the rules. Their job is more about handling day-to-day numbers and making sure everything is in order.

On the other hand, FP&A professionals look at financial data to find insights. These insights help shape the company's strategy. This means they not only understand the numbers.

They also think about what these numbers might mean for the future to help guide the company's decisions.

Example: *Let's say a traditional accountant (Mr Brooks) and an FP&A professional (Mr Cook) are looking at the same set of financial figures for a company that sells outdoor gear.*

Accountant's Mindset

Mr Brooks checks that all sales and expense figures are recorded correctly for the past quarter. He ensures all transactions comply with financial laws and standards and prepares financial reports.

His focus is mainly on what happened in the past. He makes sure everything is accurate and accounted for.

FP&A Mindset

Mr Cook uses the same figures but starts analysing trends. Such as an increase in sales in the spring season due to more hiking activities.

He forecasts future sales based on these trends, economic forecasts, and market conditions. For example, a rising interest in outdoor activities.

Mr Cook advises investing more in marketing during the spring and developing new hiking products to boost future sales. This strategic thinking helps the company plan for growth and adapt to changing market demands.

Notice that FP&A's role goes beyond just looking at numbers; they use them to guide strategic business decisions.

3. From Detail-Oriented to Big Picture Thinking:

The accountant focuses on the small, detailed parts of financial data, making sure everything is correct and in order.

FP&A, on the other hand, looks at the big picture.

They consider how different parts of the company work together and how they all impact finances, helping to guide broader business strategies.

Example Scenario: *Monthly Expense Reporting*

Accountant's Mindset

Mr Brooks is an accountant at a medium-sized retail company who is reviewing monthly expenses. He notices a discrepancy in the utility's expenses across two similar-sized store locations: one store's electricity costs are slightly higher than the others by a small margin of $150.

Mr Brooks delves into minute details. He goes and reviews meter readings, checks the number of operational hours, and compares this month's usage to the same month in the previous year. He fusses over this small difference, investigating whether it's due to an error in billing, differences in store equipment, or unauthorised usage.

FP&A Mindset

On the other hand, let's say Mr Cook an FP&A professional also reviews these reports. He views the $150 difference in a broader context.

He considers factors such as whether the slightly higher cost was due to a necessary increase in lighting for a marketing display. If yes did that boost sales?

Or could the seasonal variations justify the expense?

His focus is more on how these costs impact overall financial health and business strategy rather than the specific details of the bills themselves.

In this example, the accountant is concerned with meticulous attention to detail. In contrast, the FP&A professional accepts some level of variability if it aligns with overall strategic goals.

4. Risk Aversion to Comfort with Ambiguity

Accountants usually work in settings where accuracy is critical. And there's little tolerance for mistakes because their reports need to be very precise.

However, moving into FP&A means getting comfortable with uncertainty.

FP&A often has to make decisions with incomplete information. And manage the risks that come with that.

They need to be good at explaining these risks and their potential impacts to others in the company.

Example: *Glencore is a retail company planning its inventory for the upcoming holiday season*

Accountants Side

Mr. Brooks will make sure every detail in the inventory records is perfectly correct, down to the last item. He focuses on checking that all past records of inventory, costs, and sales match up exactly without any errors.

His reports will strictly follow all the financial rules.

FP&A Side

Mr Cook at the same company, facing the upcoming holiday season, needs to decide how much inventory to stock.

Unlike Mr Cook, Mr Brook does not have the perfect data about future sales because this depends on unpredictable holiday shopping trends.

Mr Cook uses last year's sales data and even some assumptions about consumer behaviour to forecast sales. Based on this forecast (which contains a high level of ambiguity). He makes recommendations on inventory levels.

In this example, Mr Cook manages the risk that the forecast could be wrong perhaps leading to either excess stock if sales are lower than expected. Or missed opportunities if sales exceed forecasts.

He needs to communicate these risks to the company's management.

Explaining the potential financial impacts and preparing strategies for different outcomes.

For Example, promotional tactics to move excess inventory or quick reorder strategies for stock shortages.

5. Silos to Cross-Functional Collaboration

Traditional Accountants often work in a specific, separate part of the company. They focus just on accounting and finance.

FP&A professionals need to work with different departments across the company.

They blend various business needs and viewpoints into their plans and analyses. This helps them provide more comprehensive and strategic financial advice.

Example: *Budget Planning Process*

Traditional Accountant's Role:

In a large electronics manufacturing company, Mr Brooks works primarily within the finance department. He focuses on aligning the budget figures with historical spending and revenues. And typically handles the numerical accuracy of budget entries, ensures compliance with financial regulations. And prepare reports that are mainly used internally within the finance department.

FP&A Professional's Role:

Mr Cook in the same company would approach the budget planning process differently. He would start by collaborating with various departments. Such as marketing, sales, production, and R&D. To understand their financial needs and strategic goals for the upcoming year.

For instance, if the marketing department wants to launch a new advertising campaign. Mr Cook will analyse how this expense fits into the overall company budget. And what the expected return on investment (ROI) might be.

He will integrate feedback + data from these departments to create a comprehensive plan that supports company-wide objectives.

In this example, Mr Cook goes beyond just handling numbers.

By actively engaging with different parts of the company. He ensures that the financial planning supports all departments' goals and the company's overall strategy.

This approach helps in making more informed and effective financial decisions that's aligned with company goals and objectives.

6. Data to Insights

Before getting into the difference in Mindset.

Let's first understand the Data to Insights Mountain. The "Data to Insight Mountain" is a framework that helps in understanding how data can be transformed into actionable insights.

This process is often visualized as a journey up a mountain.

Where each stage represents a deeper level of understanding and strategic value.
The stages usually include the "What", "Why", and "So What" of data analysis:

From Data to Insights

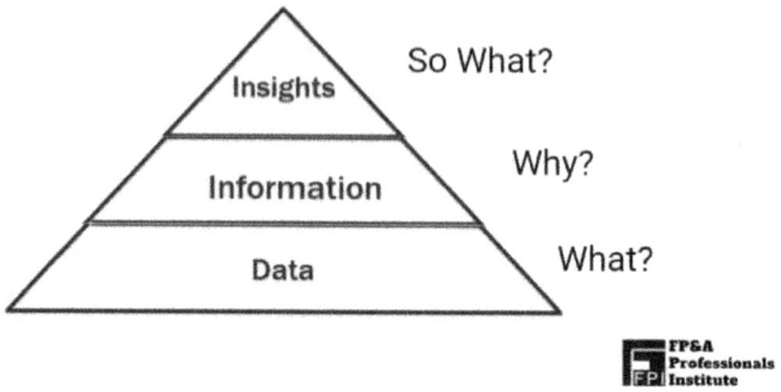

1. **The What (Descriptive Analysis):** This is the base of the mountain and involves describing what the data shows. At this stage, you're simply reporting the facts or observations from the data such as sales numbers, website traffic, or operational costs.

2. **The Why (Diagnostic Analysis):** Moving up the mountain, you start analysing why things are the way they are. This involves looking for patterns, trends, or anomalies in the data. The focus here is on causality and correlations.

   For example, you might analyse why sales spiked in a particular quarter by looking at marketing activities, economic conditions, or changes in consumer behaviour.

3. **The "So What" (Prescriptive and Predictive Analysis):** At the peak of the mountain, you address the "So What" of the analysis. This stage is about understanding what the implications of the data are and what actions should be taken as a result. It involves making predictions about future trends and offering recommendations on how the business should respond.

   For example, if the data shows a declining trend in product sales.

The "So What" could involve strategic recommendations. Recommendations could be for product improvements, increased marketing efforts, or adjusting pricing strategies.

Each step builds on the previous one, requiring more sophisticated analysis and deeper understanding.

The goal is to not just understand the past or present but to use that understanding to drive better decisions for the future.

This model emphasises the importance of not stopping at data collection or basic analysis. But instead pushing forward to derive real, actionable insights that can have an impact on the business.

Accountants and FP&A professionals approach data differently.

Of course, it's shaped by the unique demands of their roles.

Accountants have a data mindset focused on the "What" part of the Data to Insights Mountain model.

They focus on Precision and compliance, where every number must be exact.

In contrast, FP&A professionals prioritise insights, using the same data to forecast future trends and guide business decisions. Their work involves interpreting data within broader business contexts, assessing potential impacts, and suggesting actionable insights.

This shift from precise data handling to actionable insight is crucial in FP&A roles

How can we do that?

So here is a technique called the 5 Why Technique

What is the 5 Why Technique

The 5 Whys method is a technique that was developed by Sakichi Toyota (the founder of Toyota), as part of the Toyota Production System.

The idea is that by asking "why" five times, you can peel away the layers and reach the root cause of a problem.

The 5 Whys method is based on the principle that most problems have multiple causes.

And that solving the root cause can prevent the problem from happening again.

How to use the 5 Whys method?

To use the 5 Whys method, you need to define the problem clearly and concisely.

Making sure everyone involved agrees on what the problem is.

Then, ask "why" the problem occurred and write down the answer.

If the answer is not the root cause, keep asking "why" until you reach the root cause.

Or run out of logical answers.

Verify that the root cause is valid and not based on opinions or guesses by using data, evidence, or experiments to support your conclusion.

Finally, identify and implement corrective actions to address the root cause and prevent the problem from recurring.

Example of 5 Why Technique

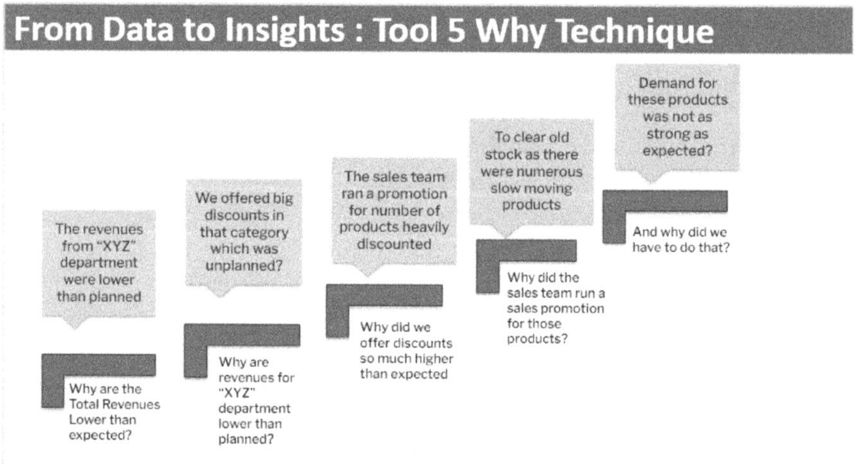

7. From Accounting Jargon to Simple Language

Accountants and FP&A professionals differ significantly in their communication styles. Especially in how they present financial information.

Accountants typically use technical jargon that aligns with accounting standards which is familiar to those within the finance and audit fields.

Their language is often detailed and precise focusing on compliance and historical accuracy.

This specialised vocabulary is crucial for ensuring clarity and consistency in financial reports. However, it can be unclear to those outside the accounting and finance field.

On the flip side, FP&A professionals prioritise simplifying complex financial concepts. This involves using less technical language and more relatable terms. This communication approach not only enhances understanding but also supports more effective decision-making across the business.

When discussing budget variances in a company meeting. Here is an example to illustrate the difference in communication styles between an accountant and an FP&A professional.

Accountant's Explanation:

"Upon reviewing the quarterly financial statements, we noted a variance of 5% in operational costs against the budget. This was primarily driven by an accrual accounting adjustment for utilities and rent that were not forecasted in our initial budget projections, aligned with the Generally Accepted Accounting Principles (GAAP)."

FP&A Professional's Explanation:

"In this quarter, our operating costs went up slightly more than expected—by about 5%. This increase was mostly due to higher utility and rent expenses that we hadn't planned for. Looking ahead, we might consider adjusting our budget forecasts to manage these costs better and avoid similar surprises."

In this example:

- The accountant focuses on precise terms like "variance" and "accrual" accounting adjustment. Sticking closely to standards like GAAP, which are essential for accurate financial reporting but can be too technical for non-experts.

- The FP&A professional simplifies the explanation by focusing on the broader impact. This is more accessible and immediately useful for decision-making by non-finance managers. They translate the accounting jargon into simple and understandable language that helps guide business actions.

Here's a table of common accounting jargon simplified into more accessible language.

Accounting Jargon	***Simplified Explanation***
Accruals	*Money earned or spent that hasn't been recorded yet.*
Capital Expenditure	*Money spent on buying or fixing long-term assets like buildings or equipment.*
Depreciation	*The decrease in the value of an asset over time.*
Amortization	*The gradual reduction of a debt or the cost of an intangible asset over a set period.*
EBITDA	*Profits before considering costs like interest, taxes, and asset value loss.*
Net Income	*The total profit after all expenses are subtracted.*
Accounts Receivable (AR)	*Money that customers owe the company.*
Accounts Payable (AP)	*Money that the company owes to suppliers or creditors.*
Balance Sheet	*A snapshot of a company's financial situation, showing what it owns and owes.*
Cash Flow	*The total amount of money being transferred in and out of a business.*
Equity	*The value of ownership interest in the company, calculated as total assets minus total liabilities.*
Deferred Revenue	*Money received for goods or services which have not yet been delivered or completed.*
Leverage	*Using borrowed money to increase the potential return of an investment.*
Phasing	*Adjusting the timing of expenses or revenues to better align with financial reporting periods. For example, spreading out the recognition of a large expense over multiple periods instead of recording it all at once.*
One-Timers	*Non-recurring or exceptional items that do not reflect the ongoing operations of a business, such as a one-time sale of assets or an unexpected legal settlement. These items are typically excluded from regular financial analysis to provide a clearer picture of the company's performance.*

Contingent Liabilities	*Potential future obligations or debts that may arise depending on the outcome of uncertain future events, such as pending lawsuits.*
Assets	Resources *owned by a company that have economic value and can be used to generate future benefits. Examples include cash, inventory, equipment, and buildings.*
Liabilities	*Obligations or debts that a company owes to external parties, arising from past transactions or events. Examples include accounts payable, loans, bonds, and accrued expenses.*

8. From Building Process to Building Relationships

Accounting Mindset: Process Orientation

An accountant's mindset revolves around following established procedures, maintaining financial controls, and producing accurate and timely reports.

Interactions with other teams and departments are often limited to clarifying transactions, verifying data, and ensuring compliance with financial regulations.

FP&A Mindset: Relationship Building

While FP&A emphasises relationship building as a key aspect of their role.

While they still rely on accurate financial data and processes. FP&A's focus extends beyond numbers to understanding the broader business context and collaborating with stakeholders across different departments.

FP&A professionals actively engage with colleagues in operations, sales, marketing, and other areas. They do this to gather insights, understand business drivers, and align financial plans with strategic objectives.

They use these cross-functional relationships to gain access to valuable data, solicit input on forecasting assumptions, and communicate financial insights effectively.

Here is an example: Scenario: Budget Planning Meeting

Accounting Mindset (Process Orientation):

During a budget planning meeting, the accounting team presents a detailed breakdown of historical expenses and revenues. They focus on ensuring that the budget follows financial regulations and internal controls, with an emphasis on accuracy and compliance.

Discussions primarily revolve around fine-tuning budget line items based on past trends and adjusting figures to meet predefined targets.

The accounting team's interactions with other departments are transactional.

With limited engagement beyond verifying financial data and ensuring adherence to budgetary constraints.

FP&A Mindset (Relationship Building):

In the same budget planning meeting, the FP&A team takes a more holistic approach.

They begin by building relationships with department heads and key stakeholders across the organisation. Seeking to understand their strategic goals, operational challenges, and growth opportunities.

Through open dialogue and collaborative discussions. The FP&A team gathers insights into business drivers, market dynamics, and emerging trends that could impact the budget. They leverage these relationships to develop a comprehensive plan that aligns with the company's needs.

Throughout the process, the FP&A team maintains ongoing communication with department heads. They provide regular updates, soliciting feedback, and fostering a sense of ownership and accountability for the budgetary decisions.

Key Takeaways:

- On one side the accounting team focuses on ensuring procedural adherence and financial accuracy.
- While on the other side, the FP&A team prioritises relationship building to gather insights and align the budget with strategic goals. By encouraging collaborative relationships with stakeholders.
- The FP&A team can develop a more informed and forward-looking budget.

- The FP&A mindset of relationship building helps proactive decision-making and strategic alignment across the organisation. This ultimately helps drive business performance and success.

9. From Numbers to Stories

Accounting Mindset: Numbers Orientation

Accountants are used to recording transactions, reconciling accounts, and generating financial statements. Their mindset revolves around ensuring the accuracy and integrity of numerical data. With an emphasis on precision and compliance.

Interactions with others often centre around clarifying financial figures, reconciling discrepancies, and ensuring that financial reports are error-free and comply with accounting principles.

FP&A Mindset: Telling Stories

FP&A professionals adopt a storytelling approach to financial analysis and reporting.

While they still rely on accurate numerical data. Their focus extends beyond the numbers. They craft narratives that provide context, insight, and meaning.

FP&A professionals use financial data to tell compelling stories about the company's performance, trends, and future outlook.

They use visualisation tools and presentations to convey complex financial information in a clear, engaging, and actionable manner.

Example Scenario: Quarterly Business Review Meeting

Numbers Orientation (Accounting Mindset):

In a quarterly business review meeting led by the accounting team.

The focus is primarily on presenting financial statements and numerical data. The discussion revolves around line-item budgets, actual expenses, revenue figures, and variances. The accounting team provides detailed reports with graphs and charts showing trends and performance metrics.

Interactions with stakeholders are transactional, with a focus on explaining the numbers and reconciling discrepancies

Telling Stories (FP&A Mindset):

In the same quarterly business review meeting led by the FP&A team.

The approach is different. Instead of just presenting numbers, the FP&A team tells a story about the company's performance and future outlook. They begin by providing context, discussing market trends, competitive landscape, and business initiatives.

Then, they weave together data with insights to paint a holistic picture of the business landscape. They highlight key achievements, challenges, and opportunities, using real-life examples and anecdotes to bring the data to life.

Through storytelling, they engage stakeholders emotionally and intellectually, leading to a deeper understanding of the company's performance and strategic direction.

Key takeaways:

- The accounting team focuses on presenting numerical data.
- The FP&A team uses storytelling to provide context, insight, and meaning behind the numbers. By telling stories, the FP&A team can engage stakeholders more effectively, drive alignment around strategic objectives, and inspire action.
- This helps the FP&A team to transform complex financial data into actionable insights that drive business performance.

10. From Email to Face to Face

In many organisations, email is the primary mode of communication for sharing information, updates, and requests.

It offers the convenience of asynchronous communication. That's allowing individuals to send messages at their convenience and receive responses at a later time.

Email communication in FP&A often involves sharing reports, analysis, and requests for information or updates. While email is efficient for disseminating information to multiple recipients and documenting conversations.

It can lack the personal touch and real-time interaction of face-to-face communication.

Face-to-Face Interaction:

Face-to-face interaction involves direct, in-person communication between individuals or groups.

Face-to-face interactions occur during meetings, presentations, workshops, and informal discussions. These interactions provide opportunities for deeper engagement, active participation, and collaboration.

Face-to-face communication allows for nuances such as body language, tone of voice, and facial expressions to be conveyed, enhancing understanding and fostering stronger relationships.

It also facilitates brainstorming, problem-solving, and decision-making in real time, leading to more effective outcomes.

Here's an example Scenario: Quarterly Forecast Review Meeting

Email Communication:

In the past, the FP&A team would send out a detailed email to department heads requesting input for the quarterly forecast.

The email would include templates for financial projections and instructions on how to fill them out.

Department heads would then respond via email with their forecasts, which the FP&A team would compile and analyse.

While this method was efficient in gathering data, it lacked the opportunity for real-time discussion and collaboration.

Face-to-Face Interaction:

In the current approach, the FP&A team schedules a face-to-face meeting with department heads to review the quarterly forecast.

During the meeting, the FP&A team presents an overview of the current financial performance. They facilitate a discussion where department heads can share their insights, assumptions, and concerns regarding their forecasts.

The meeting allows for questions to be asked, clarifications to be made, and adjustments to be discussed collaboratively.

By engaging in face-to-face interactions, the FP&A team can better understand the nuances of each department's forecasts. And ensure alignment with overall business objectives.

Key Differences and Benefits:

Relationship Building: Face-to-face meetings creates stronger relationships between the FP&A team and department heads, as well as among department heads themselves. Personal interactions build trust and rapport, leading to more open communication and collaboration.

Clarity and Understanding: In face-to-face meetings, participants can ask questions, seek clarification, and provide the context in real time, leading to better understanding and alignment of forecasts. Complex financial concepts can be explained more effectively, reducing misunderstandings.

Engagement and Collaboration: Face-to-face interactions encourage active participation and collaboration among participants, leading to richer discussions and better-informed decision-making. Participants can brainstorm ideas, share insights, and work together to address challenges and opportunities.

Conflict Resolution: Face-to-face communication allows for conflicts or disagreements to be addressed promptly and constructively as individuals can engage in dialogue, express concerns, and seek resolutions together. This creates a culture of transparency, respect, and problem-solving within the organisation.

Overall, face-to-face interactions enhance the quality of communication, collaboration, and decision-making in FP&A, leading to more effective forecasting and strategic planning processes.

11. From Challenging to Coaching

The Challenging Approach:

In a challenging approach, we may primarily focus on identifying errors, discrepancies, or areas for improvement in financial analysis or decision-making.

This approach may involve questioning assumptions, scrutinising data, and challenging the validity of conclusions or recommendations. While the intent may be to drive rigour and accountability. A challenging approach can sometimes be perceived as confrontational or argumentative. And potentially hampering collaboration and trust among team members.

The Coaching Approach:

On the other hand, a coaching approach emphasises guiding and developing team members to reach their full potential.

FP&A professionals can adopt a supportive stance. By providing constructive feedback, mentoring, and guidance to help individuals grow and excel in their roles.

This approach involves active listening, asking open-ended questions, and offering insights and perspectives to help team members overcome challenges, develop new skills, and achieve their goals.

By promoting a coaching culture. FP&A professionals empower team members to take ownership of their development and performance. This usually leads to greater engagement, job satisfaction, and productivity.

Here is an Example:

The Challenging Approach:

In the past, during a budget meeting.

The FP&A analyst took a challenging approach when discussing budget assumptions with the sales manager, John.

The analyst questioned the sales projections provided by John.

Pointing out discrepancies and challenging the feasibility of his revenue targets.

While the intent was to ensure accuracy and alignment with overall financial goals, the interaction came across as confrontational and adversarial.

The Coaching Approach:

In the current approach, during the same budget planning meeting. The FP&A analyst adopts a coaching approach.

When discussing budget assumptions with John, the sales manager.

Instead of questioning John's projections, the analyst starts by expressing appreciation for the insights provided by John. And acknowledging the challenges faced by the sales team.

They then engage in a collaborative discussion. Asking open-ended questions to understand the factors influencing sales projections and offering support and guidance where needed. The analyst works with John to explore opportunities for improving forecasting accuracy and aligning revenue targets with business objectives.

Key Differences and Benefits:

Empowerment: The coaching approach empowers John to share his insights and concerns openly. This fosters a sense of ownership and accountability for the sales projections.

Collaboration: By adopting the coaching stance, FP&A builds a collaborative relationship with Sales. They work together to identify solutions and strategies for achieving revenue targets and addressing potential challenges.

Trust and Rapport: The coaching approach builds trust and rapport between the FP&A and Sales. John feels valued and respected, knowing that his input is valued. And that the FP&A analyst is committed to supporting his success.

Long-Term Impact: Coaching has a lasting impact on the relationship between the FP&A and Sales team. By encouraging open communication and collaboration, they develop a stronger partnership. This leads to more accurate forecasting, better decision-making, and improved financial performance.

Overall, transitioning from a challenging approach to coaching. It leads to a culture of collaboration, trust, and mutual respect, driving better outcomes for the organisation.

12. From Telling to Influencing

The Telling Approach:

FP&A professionals may primarily focus on presenting financial data and analysis without considering the broader implications or influencing business decisions.

This approach involves conveying information in a straightforward manner without actively seeking to persuade or shape outcomes.

While telling may be effective in communicating facts and figures, it may not lead to meaningful engagement or action from stakeholders.

Influencing Approach:

An influencing approach emphasises shaping perceptions, attitudes, and behaviours to drive desired outcomes.

FP&A professionals adopt a proactive stance, leveraging their expertise, insights, and interpersonal skills to influence decision-making.

This approach involves framing financial data in a compelling narrative, building credibility and trust, and rallying support for proposed initiatives or recommendations.

By influencing stakeholders' perceptions and priorities, FP&A professionals can drive alignment, commitment, and action towards achieving organisational goals.

Example:

The Telling Approach:

In the past, during a budget presentation, the FP&A manager simply presented the financial figures and analysis to the executive team.

The manager outlined the budget assumptions, highlighted key metrics, and provided insights into the company's financial performance.

While the presentation was informative, it lacked a compelling narrative or call to action to influence decision-making.

The Influencing Approach:

In the current approach, during the same budget presentation, The FP&A manager engages the executive team to drive alignment around key initiatives. Instead of simply presenting numbers, the manager starts by framing the budget in the context of the company's strategic objectives.

Weaving a narrative that highlights the challenges and opportunities facing the organisation. Next, emphasising the need for investments and resource allocation to drive growth and innovation.

The manager uses communication techniques, storytelling and data visualisation to build credibility and inspire action from the executive team.

Key Differences and Benefits:

Strategic Alignment: The influencing approach ensures that the budget is strategically aligned with the company's goals and priorities. By framing the budget within a strategic narrative, the FP&A manager garners support and buy-in from the executive team for proposed initiatives and investments.

Stakeholder Engagement: Influencing leads to meaningful engagement and collaboration with stakeholders. This leads to more informed decision-making and better outcomes. By actively seeking input and addressing concerns, the FP&A manager creates a sense of ownership and commitment among the executive team.

Driving Change: Influencing enables the FP&A manager to drive change and innovation within the organisation. By advocating for new approaches or investments, they inspire action and mobilize resources towards achieving desired outcomes.

Building Relationships: An influencing approach builds trust and rapport with stakeholders, enhancing the credibility and effectiveness of the FP&A manager. By establishing themselves as a trusted advisor and thought leader, they can exert greater influence over decision-making processes and outcomes.

Overall moving from the telling approach to influencing creates a big impact. It helps FP&A to shape perceptions, drive change, and achieve organisational success.

Now that we have understood the mindset shift, in Chapter 4 let's dive into the specific roles and responsibilities within FP&A.

Section 2

Understanding The FP&A Role

Chapter 4
FP&A Roles And Responsibilities

In this chapter, we will explore the different types of FP&A roles.

Common FP&A positions from analysts to senior executives. Also, we will discuss typical FP&A job responsibilities, review sample job descriptions. And debunk common myths about the profession.

7 Most Common FP&A Roles and Designations

Being aware of these 7 common FP&A designations. And the related requirements can help you assess the FP&A job profile better.

1. FP&A Associate / Intern

FP&A associate is responsible for supporting the FP&A team. Day to day tasks usually include data entry, report generation, presentations update and supporting the budgets.

2. FP&A Analyst / FP&A Sr Analyst / FP&A Assistant Manager

The FP&A Analyst is responsible to analyse data, develop financial models that help make informed decisions. Also, they support the preparation of budgets, forecasts, and management reports.

3. FP&A Manager / FP&A Senior Manager

The FP&A manager is responsible for managing a team of analysts and providing financial insights and recommendations to senior leadership.

4. FP&A Director / Vice President, FP&A

The FP&A director / VP is responsible for leading the FP&A function. This includes setting direction and providing insights and recommendations to senior leadership.

5. FP&A Consultant

Consultant is an external expert who works with a variety of clients.

Meaning they don't work inside the organisation and are typically brought in for specific needs. They help improve processes, solve problems, and develop recommendations. All this is aimed to improving business performance.

6. FP&A specialist / Subject Matter Expert (SME)

The FP&A specialist is like a consultant but working inside the organisation. He/she is an expert who has a deep understanding of one function or domain or tool. And is responsible for providing specialised support within an organisation.

7. Finance Business Partner

The role of an FP&A Business Partner involves working with internal stakeholders on FP&A activities. They're specialised in one function, for example, Sales Finance Business Partner, Supply Chain Finance Business Partner, or Marketing Finance Business Partner.

Below are side by side comparisons of the key activities of the 3 Core FP&A roles at different levels:

FP&A Analyst	***FP&A Manager***	***FP&A Director***
The FP&A Analyst serves as the foundational role in the FP&A department. Primary responsibilities include. • *Collecting and Analysing data,* • *Preparing Reports, and* • *Assist in the creation of budget and forecast models.* • *Analysts also perform variance analysis, comparing actual performance to budgeted targets to identify discrepancies*	*Managers hold a central role in steering the direction of their organisations.* *They oversee the daily operations of the FP&A teams, including.* • *Managing the reporting process,* • *Leading the budgeting and forecasting cycles, and* • *Providing actionable financial insights to support decisions.*	*The director operates at a strategic level, often reporting directly to the CFO.* *Involves a high degree of leadership, overseeing the FP&A team and ensuring that all financial analysis and reporting support the company's long-term strategy.* *The director also plays a crucial role in strategic planning sessions, offering*

and areas for improvement. *The analyst role is pivotal in providing the necessary data-driven insights that inform more decisions made by senior management.*	*This role requires collaboration with various departments to ensure plans and forecasts align with business objectives.* *Managers are responsible for improving processes and tools to enhance the efficiency of forecasts and reports.*	*insights and recommendations that shape corporate policies and objectives.* *Beyond internal management, the FP&A Director may interact with stakeholders, providing them with an understanding of the company's financial position and progress towards its goals.*

	FP&A Analyst	FP&A Manager	FP&A Lead
Role	Analyst, Sr Analyst, Assistant Mgr	FP&A Manager, Sr Manager, AGM, AVP	FP&A Director, Vice President
Reporting to	FP&A Manager, Sr Manager, AGM, Associate Director	FP&A Director, Vice President	CFO
Key activities	Develop financial models and analyse them to support strategic initiatives. Maintain FP&A reporting tools Monthly financial close process Month end Quarter end decks	Manage the various FP&A processes. Drive Special projects and analysis Support ad-hoc requests from senior management. Partner with business and functions to drive business initiatives. Identify, implement, and deliver key operational efficiencies.	Developing the budget guidelines Timely delivery of the budget, forecasts and supporting analysis Act as a sounding board when making commercial decisions and formulating strategy

FP&A Professionals Institute

Sample Job Descriptions of FP&A Roles

FP&A Analyst Job Description

Objective:

FP&A Analyst will support financial planning, budgeting, forecasting, and analysis to assist the company in optimising financial performance and strategic decision-making.

Key Responsibilities:

- *Assist in the monthly financial reporting and forecasting processes.*
- *Prepare budgets, forecasts, and financial models to support decision-making.*
- *Analyse financial data and trends to provide actionable insights.*
- *Collaborate with various departments to gather and analyse financial information.*
- *Support the preparation of presentations and reports for senior management.*

Qualifications:

- CA, CMA, CPA, *bachelor's in finance,* Accounting, Economics, *related field.*
- 1-3 *years of experience in financial analysis or a similar role.*
- *Strong analytical skills and proficiency with* Excel *and financial modelling.*
- *Excellent communication and interpersonal skills.*

Sample FP&A Manager Job Description

Objective:

The FP&A Manager will lead financial planning, budgeting, and forecasting efforts, driving the analytical framework for strategic business decisions.

Key Responsibilities:

- *Manage the FP&A processes across the company.*
- *Oversee the creation and maintenance of detailed budgets, financial models, and forecasts.*
- *Provide insights and recommendations to optimise business performance.*

- *Lead the budgeting process, engaging with department heads to ensure alignment with strategic objectives.*
- *Develop and present management reports to senior executives.*

Qualifications:

- *CA, CMA, CPA, bachelor's or master's in finance, Accounting, or related field.*
- *5+ years of experience in financial planning and analysis, with at least 2 years in a management role.*
- *Strong leadership skills and experience in managing a team.*
- *Advanced skills in Excel and financial software systems.*

Sample FP&A Director / FP&A Head Job Description

Objective:

The Director of FP&A will lead the company's financial planning and strategic analysis, guiding long-term financial forecasts and providing insights to inform executive-level decision-making.

Key Responsibilities:

- *Direct the development of comprehensive forecasts, reports, and budgets.*
- *Oversee the analysis of data and market trends to support strategic initiatives.*
- *Lead, develop, and mentor the FP&A team.*
- *Collaborate with senior leadership to align financial management with short- and long-term financial planning and projections.*
- *Communicate critical financial matters to the board of directors and C-suite executives.*

Qualifications:

- *CA, CPA, CMA, master's in business administration, Finance, or related field.*

- *10+ years of progressive experience in FP&A, with significant leadership experience.*
- *Demonstrated ability to lead a financial team with strategic oversight.*
- *Exceptional communication and leadership skills.*

Disclaimer:

- Please note that the job descriptions provided in this chapter are illustrative and intended to serve as general templates.
- Actual job descriptions for FP&A roles can vary significantly from company to company, depending on specific industry requirements, company size, corporate culture, and other factors.
- It's important for both job seekers and employers to tailor these templates to reflect the unique needs and expectations of their specific organisational contexts.

Looking at the three job descriptions for FP&A roles at different levels – Analyst, Manager, and Director. We can observe a clear progression in responsibilities, expectations, and required qualifications.

FP&A Analyst

The FP&A Analyst role is heavily concentrated on supporting day-to-day tasks.

Tasks like reporting, collecting budget inputs, and basic financial analysis. The responsibilities are executional with a strong emphasis on data gathering, number crunching, and providing support to senior staff.

Candidates are expected to have foundational finance or accounting knowledge, strong analytical capabilities, and proficiency in tools like Excel. This position typically requires a few years of experience or could even be suitable for recent graduates with relevant internships.

FP&A Manager

Moving up to the Manager level.

The role transitions from support to leadership within the FP&A function. The Manager oversees the FP&A processes such as the financial planning cycles (budgets and forecasts) and directly contributes to strategic decision-making.

This position demands a higher level of expertise. This includes advanced financial modelling skills and the ability to manage a team. Experience-wise, candidates need several years in financial roles with a proven track record of managing processes + teams.

Director of FP&A

At the Director level, the scope becomes more strategic than tactical.

This role involves leading the entire FP&A function. Plan and oversee budgets, forecasts and analyses that influence the company's strategic directions. The Director of FP&A also plays a key role in advising senior management and often interacts with the board of directors.

This position requires extensive experience. Often more than a decade, with a deep understanding of business and financial strategies. Leadership skills are crucial. And so is the ability to communicate complex financial information to non-financial stakeholders.

Comments:

As we move up the hierarchy from Analyst to Director.

There is a notable shift from executing specific tasks to managing broad strategic functions. Each role builds upon the skills and experiences of the previous one. But with added layers of complexity and leadership responsibilities.

The progression also underscores the need for continuous skill development.

For instance, an Analyst mastering Excel and basic financial modelling may evolve into a manager who must handle a team of FP&A analysts and eventually a director who must lead the FP&A Function.

Another key observation is the increasing level of strategic influence each role holds. While an Analyst might influence decisions through data and insight sharing, a director's role is vital in shaping company-wide strategy. Having explored job descriptions at different levels within the FP&A hierarchy.

Let's now shift our focus to examine how these roles vary across organisations of different sizes, from small startups to large multinational corporations.

Types of FP&A Roles in Different Organisations

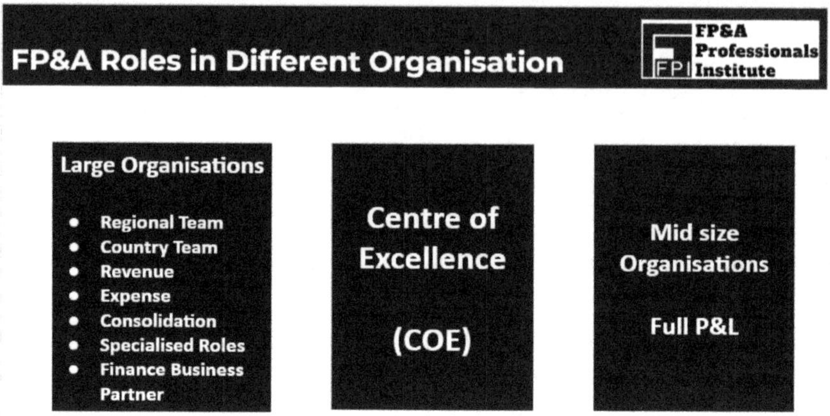

Large Organisations

In large organisations, FP&A roles are typically more specialised and hierarchical.

Usually, these big organisations might have a complex structure with FP&A teams divided by region, country, or product line, each with specific revenue and expense responsibilities.

In a large organisation you will most likely be looking at one specific area. This could be a specific expense line, a specific product or service, or Revenues for a particular segment. You could also be looking at an area, region, or country.

Or you could be at the corporate office consolidating the different countries and region plans and reports.

Mid-Sized Organisation

FP&A roles in mid-sized organisation often require a broader range of responsibilities across the entire profit and loss (P&L). Meaning these roles typically give Full P&L visibility. This is usually not possible in a large organisation.

Professionals in these roles handle comprehensive oversight for the entire organisation or significant business segments.

FP&A professionals in mid-sized firms may have to perform multiple roles that in larger organisations would be handled by several specialists, such as managing budgets, forecasts, and strategic planning simultaneously.

Smaller Organisations

In smaller organisation, FP&A roles are usually less specialised. One or two individuals might perform all FP&A functions. This provides a unique opportunity to handle a wide array of FP&A tasks from strategic planning to detailed financial analysis.

Centre of Excellence (COE) or Shared Service Units:

Centres of Excellence (COEs) or Shared Services Units in FP&A are getting increasingly popular. They are recognised for their ability to enhance the efficiency and effectiveness of finance operations in big organisations.

They focus on pooling expertise in specific areas of finance. And provide high-quality analytical support and advisory services.

Meanwhile, they centralise routine and transactional activities such as budgeting and financial reporting. The idea is to reduce costs and improve service delivery standards.

The COE model not only streamlines processes. It also allows FP&A teams to focus more on strategic activities and less on admin tasks.

Key factors driving the formation of COEs in organisations.

When forming Centres of Excellence (COEs) organisations typically consider factors such as strategic alignment, expertise concentration, and efficiency gains.

The structure of COEs often involves assembling a team of specialists with deep knowledge in specific financial areas like budgeting, forecasting, or FP&A tool specialists.

This setup not only streamlines processes across the organisation but also enhances the quality of financial analysis and decision-making.

COE teams work closely with various business units to ensure that financial practices align with company objectives. Often, they spearhead initiatives for process improvements and efficiency enhancements across the organisation.

The benefits of implementing COEs

- Streamlining operations and enhance the accuracy of forecasts and reporting by centralizing expertise and adopting standardized best practices.
- Cost savings through more efficient resource allocation and reduced redundancies.
- Drive improvements in decision-making quality by providing business units with deeper insights and more reliable data.

These strategic benefits help organisation respond more agilely to market changes and facilitate more informed strategic planning.

COE Real-World Examples

Johnson & Johnson, Microsoft, General Electric, and other leading companies have established FP&A COEs to streamline and enhance their finance operations globally.

For instance, Johnson & Johnson's FP&A COE focuses on standardising financial reporting and boosting the accuracy of budgeting and forecasting while Microsoft's Finance COE centralises expertise to influence strategic decisions and optimise investments.

Similarly, General Electric's Corporate FP&A COE consolidates financial reporting to support strategic decision-making.

Companies like Pfizer, Deloitte, and Siemens also have COEs dedicated to optimising financial processes, providing M&A analysis, and supporting investment strategies, respectively.

Also, banks like Citi, Barclays, Credit Suisse, JPMorgan Chase, HSBC, and Goldman Sachs have established FP&A COEs. By centralising financial expertise, these banks are better equipped to manage risks, improve operational efficiency, and align financial strategies with business objectives.

COEs play a crucial role in improving operational efficiency, financial consistency, and strategic planning across their respective global operations.

Frequently Asked Questions

Here are some frequently asked questions about working in FP&A COEs

1. What qualifications are needed to work in an FP&A COE?

Typically, qualifications include a degree in finance, accounting, economics, or business administration. Strong analytical skills, proficiency in financial modelling, and experience with financial software are also highly valued.

2. What are the main responsibilities of FP&A COE professionals? -

Responsibilities often include budgeting, forecasting, performing variance analysis, developing financial models, and providing strategic advice to management based on data analysis.

3. How does working in an FP&A COE differ from other finance roles?

Unlike day-to-day operational finance roles. FP&A COE roles focus on analysis.

This analysis can be both strategic and transactional analysis, integrating data from across the organisation to guide long-term business decisions.

4. What are the career prospects in an FP&A COE?

Given the broad exposure to business operations and strategic decision-making.

Career prospects can include advancement to senior management roles in finance, strategic planning, even general management.

5. What skills are crucial for success in an FP&A COE?

Key skills include advanced analytical abilities, expertise in financial software, strong communication skills to convey complex information and strategic thinking.

6. Is experience in finance necessary to join an FP&A COE?

While a background in finance is common many professionals in FP&A COEs come from various fields if they possess strong analytical and strategic skills.

7. What challenges might one face working in an FP&A COE?

Challenges may include managing large datasets, integrating information from disparate parts of the organisation, and the pressure of influencing high-stakes decisions.

8. How can one prepare for a role in an FP&A COE?

Preparation could include gaining certifications like CA, CMA or CPA, acquiring practical experience through internships in analysis and developing proficiency in financial modelling and data analysis tools.

9. Is the quality of work in an FP&A COE considered lower than in business-facing roles?

Not at all. The work in FP&A COEs is highly valued for its strategic impact on the organisation. Although, it might be less directly involved with day-to-day business operations. It plays a crucial role in guiding long-term financial strategies and decision-making.

10. Can work in an FP&A COE become monotonous?

While some routine tasks are involved. Such as regular reporting cycles.

The role also requires a lot of dynamic analysis, scenario planning, and strategic forecasting, which can vary significantly and be quite intellectually stimulating.

11. What is the work-life balance like in an FP&A COE?

Work-life balance can vary by company and role intensity.

However, most organisation strive to maintain a healthy balance for their employees. Periods such as fiscal year-end or quarterly reporting might require longer hours. But these are generally balanced by quieter periods.

12. How can I ensure that my work in an FP&A COE remains engaging and avoids monotony?

Seek out opportunities for involvement in diverse projects.

Such as cross-departmental initiatives or new product launches. Continuous learning and upgrading skills, such as advanced analytics or machine learning can also keep the work engaging.

13. Are there opportunities for creative problem-solving in FP&A COEs?

Absolutely. FP&A COEs often face complex financial challenges requiring innovative financial solutions and models, especially when it comes to forecasting and strategic planning.

14. What measures are in place to prevent burnout in high-pressure FP&A COE roles?

Many organisations offer support through flexible work arrangements, mental health resources, and a culture that promotes team collaboration and support. Regular training and developmental opportunities can also help maintain motivation and prevent burnout.

15. What should I do if I feel stuck in a rut in my FP&A role?

Feeling stuck in a rut in any role can be challenging, but there are several proactive steps you can take to rejuvenate your career and find renewed motivation:

- **Seek New Challenges:** Ask for different types of projects or responsibilities that can provide new challenges and learning opportunities. This can help you break the monotony and engage with your work in fresh ways.

- **Pursue Professional Development:** Consider furthering your education through certifications, workshops, or courses that are relevant to your field. This not only enhances your skills but can also open new avenues within your current role or organisation.

- **Request Feedback and Guidance:** Discuss your career aspirations and feelings of stagnation with your manager. Seek feedback on your performance and ask for guidance on potential career paths or advancement opportunities within the organisation.

- **Network Internally:** Engage with colleagues in different departments or teams. This can provide insights into other areas of the business that might interest you and could lead to opportunities for internal transfers or collaborative projects.

- **Focus on Innovation:** Try to innovate in your current role. Look for ways to improve processes, enhance reports, or introduce new tools that can increase efficiency and effectiveness in your work.

- **Assess Your Career Goals:** Sometimes feeling stuck can be a sign that your current role no longer aligns with your personal or professional goals. Reflect on what you truly want from your career and consider, if a more significant change is needed.
- **Find a Mentor:** Find someone within or outside your organisation who can provide career advice, support, and perspective. A mentor who has navigated similar challenges can offer valuable insights and encouragement.

By taking these steps, you can create more engagement and satisfaction in your role. Potentially leading to new opportunities that reignite your passion for your work in FP&A.

After looking at FP&A roles in different sizes of organisation, let's now address and debunk some common myths surrounding the FP&A function.

9 Common Myths about FP&A roles

Despite the importance of FP&A. There are many myths and misconceptions about FP&A that can lead to misunderstandings about the work that FP&A professionals do.

Here are the top 9 myths about FP&A roles:

Myth #1: FP&A is just about creating budgets.

While budgeting is certainly a key component of FP&A.

It is far from the only thing that FP&A professionals do; In addition to creating budgets. FP&A professionals are also responsible for analysing and interpreting financial data, and developing financial models, forecasts and providing insights and recommendations to decision-makers.

Myth #2: FP&A is only for finance professionals.

While it is true that many FP&A professionals have a background in finance or accounting.

This is not a requirement for the role. In fact, many FP&A professionals come from diverse backgrounds, such as economics, business, or even engineering. What is important for an FP&A role is the ability to analyse and interpret financial data, understand business operations, and communicate effectively with decision-makers.

Myth #3: FP&A is a boring and mundane job.

While some aspects of FP&A work may be routine.

The role can also be quite dynamic and challenging. FP&A professionals are often at the forefront of analysing and interpreting financial data, which can inform important business decisions and strategies.

As a result, FP&A professionals can make a meaningful impact on the direction and success of the organisation.

Myth #4: FP&A is all about numbers.

While there is certainly a lot of data and numbers involved in FP&A work.

It is not all about the numbers. FP&A professionals must be able to interpret and understand the meaning and context behind the numbers and be able to communicate this effectively to decision-makers. This requires strong analytical skills, the ability to think critically + strategically and good communication.

Myth #5: FP&A is only about the past and present.

While FP&A does involve analysing and understanding historical financial data.

It is also about looking to the future. FP&A professionals are responsible for developing financial forecasts and models, which help to inform long-term planning and strategy.

Myth #6: FP&A is only about cost-cutting.

While cost management is an important aspect of FP&A.

It is not the only focus of the role. FP&A professionals are also responsible for analysing revenue and growth opportunities and for identifying ways to optimise financial performance.

Myth #7: FP&A is only for large organisations.

FP&A is a critical function for any organisation, regardless of size.

Small and medium-sized businesses also rely on FP&A to inform decision-making and strategy. And in fact, may even have a higher need for these services due to limited resources.

Myth #8: FP&A is a standalone function.

While FP&A operates as a separate function within an organisation.

It is not completely isolated. FP&A professionals work closely with other departments and teams to understand and analyse financial data. And to provide insights and recommendations that support the overall goals of the organisation.

Myth #9: FP&A is a dead-end career.

FP&A is not a dead-end career.

In fact, the skills and experience gained in an FP&A role can be highly valuable in a variety of different careers. Many FP&A professionals go on to pursue leadership roles within finance or other departments.

In this chapter, we have explored the diverse roles within FP&A (from analysts to senior executives).

We discussed the typical responsibilities associated with FP&A positions, debunked common myths about the profession, and reviewed sample job descriptions for FP&A Analyst, FP&A Manager, and Director of FP&A.

In the next chapter, we take a glimpse into the daily routine of FP&A professionals and understand the significant impact FP&A roles have on business decisions.

Chapter 5
A Day In Life Of An FP&A Professional

This chapter explores a typical day for FP&A Teams and understand how FP&A professionals navigate challenges, support their company's goals, and adapt to ever-changing business needs.

Activities In a Day

Here are some key activities FP&A usually engage in:

1. **Budget Review and Variance Analysis:** They prepare the budget. And post month-end, review actuals vs. budgeted figures to identify variances and suggest corrective actions.
2. **Financial Forecasting:** They update financial forecasts to reflect the latest position of the company's future financials.
3. **Management Reporting:** They prepare periodic reports and presentations that help senior management understand the financial status and progress of the company.
4. **Strategic Meetings:** They participate in strategic planning sessions, offering insights and recommendations based on financial data.
5. **Collaboration and Data Gathering:** They work closely with various departments to collect and analyse data essential for forecasting and budgeting.
6. **Ad Hoc Analysis:** They perform specialised, on-demand financial analysis to address urgent business questions. Or to provide insights on unexpected scenarios, supporting decision-making in real-time.
7. **Capital Investment Decisions:** Evaluate potential capital investments, assessing their financial viability, risk, and alignment with long-term goals. They model scenarios, calculate return on investment, and support decision-making with detailed financial projections.

8. **Crisis Management and Response:** They develop strategies to manage financial stability during economic downturns, including cost management initiatives and scenario planning to mitigate financial risks.

9. **Digital Transformation and Automation:** They lead initiatives to implement new technologies that enhance data processing, reporting capabilities, and analytical insights, driving efficiencies across the company.

10. **Global Expansion Strategy:** They analyse and strategise for entering new international markets, managing currency risks, ensuring compliance with financial regulations, and tailoring financial strategies to local market conditions.

Next let's look at some real-life scenarios, examples, and cases.

Real Life Scenarios and their Takeaways

Example 1: Embracing Constant Change and Ambiguity

Mr. Virat is an FP&A Manager at a mid-sized company. During the planning season he is coordinating with various business teams Here's a breakdown of a typical day:

8 AM – 9 AM	*Virat starts his day by reviewing emails and the latest draft of the company-wide financial plan.*
9 AM – 10 AM	*He meets with his team of Analysts on a standing call to discuss the timeline and deliverables for the upcoming weeks.*
10 AM – 11 AM	*His morning takes a turn. His boss Mr. Rohit (Director of FP&A) informs him that the CFO (Mr. Dhoni) has requested revisions to all assumptions for the financial plan. This request comes as the new CEO (Mr. Sachin) aims to implement more aggressive strategies.*
11 AM – 12 PM	*Virat revisits the forecasts, focusing on ROI, ROE, and ROA for various markets, and proposes simplifying the presentation to make it more accessible by reducing financial jargon.*
12 PM – 1 PM	*Lunch offers a chance for Virat to mentor a new hire (Mr. Shubhman) about navigating office dynamics, particularly the CEO-CFO relationship*

1 PM – 4 PM	*In the afternoon, Virat conducts Zoom calls with FP&A managers from different regions, discussing their financial targets.*
4 PM – 6 PM	*After compiling the inputs, Virat realises the company is likely to fall short of its income target.* *Primarily due to:* 1. *Foreign exchange rate fluctuations.* 2. *Russia-Ukraine war impact on the EMEA market* *He delegates his senior analyst (Mr. Surya) to prepare a presentation explaining this variance.*

This example shows the dynamic nature of the FP&A role, showcasing how professionals must adapt to strategic changes and communicate complex information effectively.

Here are some takeaways from the above case:

1. Navigating Change and Uncertainty:

Mr. Virat's day exemplifies the importance of flexibility which is the readiness to adapt to sudden changes in strategic direction, such as when the CFO (Mr. Dhoni) requested revisions to all financial assumptions. This requires an ability to quickly reassess and realign strategies with new senior management objectives.

2. Understanding Office Politics:

The lunch discussion about CEO-CFO dynamics highlights the need for understanding office politics. Knowing the interpersonal and interdepartmental relationships is crucial for FP&A career advancement.

3. Ability to See the Big Picture:

By coordinating with various regional FP&A managers and synthesising their inputs. Virat demonstrates the ability to maintain a broad perspective. This involves understanding how changes affect the global outlook. And how to integrate these insights into the company's overall planning.

4. Effective Communication:

The need to simplify financial presentations by reducing jargon and making them accessible shows the importance of clear communication. Being able to convey complex financial data in an understandable way is critical for ensuring that all stakeholders, regardless of their financial acumen, are on the same page.

5. Strategic Thinking and Problem Solving:

The end-of-day realisation that the company will fall short of its income targets. Quickly summarising the big picture reasons being due to exchange rate effects, and the impact of the Russia-Ukraine war. The subsequent strategy session to craft a narrative around this issue highlights the strategic thinking involved in FP&A. This shows how we must not only identify and analyse problems but also creatively develop and present solutions that align with company goals.

Example 2: Understanding Business and strategy along with Leadership and Communication Skills

8 AM – 9 AM	*Emily starts her morning by analysing overnight financial news. She updates her financial models to reflect the latest market conditions, ensuring her planning is responsive and robust.*
9 AM – 10 AM	*She holds a strategy meeting with her FP&A team to discuss the implications of the new information and adjust their approach to the upcoming planning season. Emily emphasises the need for flexibility in their models to account for economic volatility.*
10 AM – 11 AM	*An urgent meeting with the CFO and CEO has been called to discuss a major competitor's recent strategic moves. Emily presents her team's findings and engages in strategic discussions on how to adjust their company's plans to maintain a competitive edge.*
11 AM – 12 PM	*Back with her team, Emily leads the effort to pivot their planning to address the new strategic priorities. They brainstorm innovative cost optimization strategies and explore new revenue streams*
12 PM – 1 PM	*During her lunch break, Emily networks with industry peers at a local café, gathering insights into industry trends and best practices that she could integrate into her planning*
1 PM – 4 PM	*The afternoon is spent in meetings with department heads to align their plans with the revised company-wide strategy. Emily facilitates these discussions, ensuring that all departments understand their roles in the new strategy.*

4 PM – 6 PM	*Emily and her team finalise the day's work by integrating feedback into the financial plan. They develop a preliminary presentation for the senior executives, focusing on clear communication of the strategic adjustments.*

In this example Emily demonstrates strategic agility and leadership, highlighting how FP&A must continually adapt to external economic factors and internal company dynamics.

Here are Key takeaways from the above case:

1. Adaptability in Response to Market Changes:

Emily's ability to quickly assimilate new market information. And then adjusting financial models accordingly demonstrates a high level of adaptability. This skill is crucial in allowing her to keep her company's strategies aligned with external economic conditions.

2. Strategic and Cross Functional Collaboration:

Throughout the day, Emily collaborates with her team and other department heads. This ensures that the revised plans are integrated and understood across the company. This ability to facilitate effective collaboration shows the importance of teamwork. Also, it highlights FP&A's role in bridging financial insights with operational execution.

3. Leadership and Communication:

Emily's day features back-to-back strategic discussions and presentations. All this requires her to communicate complex financial data clearly and persuasively. Her leadership skills are evident as she guides her team through strategic pivots. She ensures that everyone remains on track with the new directives and that the budget reflects the company's adjusted objectives.

Example 3: Cross-Functional Collaboration

8 AM – 9 AM	*Lucas starts his day meeting with the Sales team to review the latest sales forecasts. And, to discuss potential financial impacts of upcoming product launches. He helps them understand how their numbers contribute to the company's overall goals and discusses strategies to optimise sales performance against expectations.*

9 AM - 10 AM	*Next, Lucas sits down with the Marketing department to finalise the budget for the new quarter. They go through planned marketing campaigns, evaluating their expected ROI and aligning their spending with strategic business outcomes. Lucas advises on a few cost-saving measures without compromising the effectiveness of the campaign.*
10 AM - 11 AM	*Lucas meets with the IT department. They discuss their current technology investments and upcoming needs. They explore the financial viability of proposed IT projects and how these investments align with broader business objectives. Lucas assists in prioritising projects based on their potential business impact and ROI.*
11 AM - 12 PM	*Lucas uses this time to check and reply to emails and catch up on missed phone calls.*
12 PM – 1 PM	*Lucas takes the lunch break and goes for a 20-minute walk*
1 PM – 4 PM	*Lucas spends the afternoon integrating the insights and data gathered from these meetings into the company's financial model. He updates forecasts and prepares a comprehensive report that highlights key financial insights from each department, ensuring that the executive team understands the interconnected impact of departmental actions on financial health.*
4 PM – 6 PM	*To conclude his day, Lucas presents a summary of his findings and recommendations to the executive team.*

This example shows how Lucas interacts with multiple departments throughout the day. He ensures that the financial plan is integrated across the company and aligns with strategic goals.

Here are some key takeaways:

1. Cross-Functional Collaboration:

Lucas interacted with different departments such as Sales, Marketing, and IT. This shows the importance of cross-functional collaboration in FP&A. His role in connecting these teams shows how integrated financial planning is crucially important.

2. Strategic Influence:

Each meeting Lucas has throughout the day not only allows him to gather vital data. But it also gives him an opportunity to influence departmental strategies.

His input helps ensure that departmental plans are not only aligned with each other. But they are also aligned with the company's overall goals.

This best shows the strategic influence of the FP&A role.

3. Communication Skills:

Lucas's ability to communicate complex financial concepts in ways that is understandable and actionable for non-finance departments highlights the communication skills required in FP&A. Effective communication ensures that insights are correctly interpreted and implemented.

4. Adaptability and Problem Solving:

Lucas integrates feedback and aligns departmental budgets and strategies.

His adaptability and problem-solving skills come into play. These skills are vital in managing the dynamic and sometimes conflicting needs of different business units. While still aiming for optimal financial outcomes.

5. Data Integration and Reporting:

Lucas's skill in integrating diverse data points into a coherent financial model that provides actionable insights is valuable. He prepares a comprehensive report for the executive team. This demonstrates how FP&A synthesise information to guide decision-making at the highest levels.

Example 4: Crisis Management and Response:

Sophia, the Chief Planning Officer. Her company faces a significant downturn in the market. The latest revenue projections threaten the need for widespread layoffs.

Here's how she leads her team to manage the crisis effectively:

Immediate Financial Review:

As soon as the downturn is apparent. Sophia convenes an emergency meeting with her FP&A team to review all current expenses and revenue forecasts.

They quickly identify non-essential spending that can be paused or eliminated. These are non-critical vendor contracts, planned upgrades to office facilities, and discretionary departmental budgets.

Strategic Hiring Freeze:

Sophia proposes a company-wide hiring freeze to the executive team as an immediate measure to conserve cash. She presents a detailed analysis showing how the hiring freeze, combined with natural attrition, could save the company significant payroll costs. This could prevent the company from resorting to layoffs.

Scenario Planning:

To ensure readiness for any prolonged economic impact. Sophia and her team developed multiple scenarios to forecast the potential impact of the crisis. These scenarios help the company plan for various outcomes, including worst-case and best-case scenarios.

Communication and Collaboration:

To ensure transparency and maintain morale. Sophia communicates the reasons for the hiring freeze to the entire company. She collaborates closely with HR to manage the implementation of the hiring freeze. Her team ensures that it maintains operational capabilities.

Ongoing Monitoring and Adjustment:

Sophia sets up a weekly review meeting with her team and key department heads. They continuously monitor the impact of the cost-cutting measures. They adjust their strategies in real time based on new data and market conditions, staying flexible to pivot as necessary.

Long-term Strategic Review:

Recognising the need to prepare for future uncertainties. Sophia reviews the company's policies and risk management strategies. This includes enhancing the company's liquidity reserves and diversifying its revenue streams to mitigate the impact of similar crises in the future.

Key Takeaways:

In this example, Sophia demonstrates proactive leadership, strategic thinking, and effective communication.

Her approach not only helps the company navigate through the immediate financial crisis. But also positions it for stronger financial health in the future. This case study highlights the FP&A's crucial role in crisis management.

It also shows how strategic decisions can prevent drastic measures like layoffs. And at the same time support the company's long-term stability.

Example 5: Evaluation of a Capital Investment Proposal

Martin, the Senior FP&A Manager, receives a proposal from the head of the Product Development department requesting funding for a new manufacturing facility. This investment is aimed at expanding the company's production capacity.

Here's how Martin and his FP&A team approach the evaluation:

Initial Review and Information Gathering:

- *Martin begins by conducting an initial review of the proposal.*
- *Here he understands its scope and strategic alignment with the company's long-term goals. He requests inputs for detailed projections from the Product team. This includes expected costs, revenue potential, and market analysis for the products to be manufactured.*

Financial Modelling and Risk Assessment:

- *Next Martin's team creates a financial model that simulates the potential outcomes of the investment.*
- *The model includes cash flow projections, payback periods, and different scenarios like best case, worse case, and base case. The model also includes internal rates of return (IRR), and sensitivity analyses. They assess risks such as market demand fluctuations, regulatory changes, and potential delays in construction and production ramp-up.*

Stakeholder Consultation:

- *To gather broader insights and perspectives.*
- *Martin organises a series of consultations with key stakeholders across the company, including operations, sales, marketing, and legal teams.*
- *These discussions help assess operational readiness, market entry strategies, and any legal implications of the new facility.*

External Expertise:

- *Recognising the need for specialised knowledge. Martin uses the company's consulting budget to hire an external consultancy firm to conduct a feasibility study. This study evaluates local market conditions, competition, labor market analysis, and environmental impact assessments.*

Presentation to the Executive Team:

- *With all the data and analyses in hand.*
- *Martin prepares a detailed presentation for the company's executive team. The presentation outlines the capital investment's benefits, risks, and strategic importance. It includes financial metrics and strategic fit with company objectives. Along with a proposed timeline for the investment.*

Decision-Making:

- *The executive team reviews Martin's presentation and engages in a thorough discussion about the proposed investment. Martin and the team answer questions and provide additional insights into the financial and strategic considerations.*
- *Based on the comprehensive evaluation presented, the executive team makes an informed decision to proceed with the investment.*

Implementation Oversight

- *Once the investment is approved, Martin's role shifts to overseeing the implementation process. He ensures financial controls are in place, monitors expenditures against the budget, and updates the financial models based on actual project progress and market developments.*

Key Takeaways:

In this example, Martin exemplifies the critical role of FP&A in making informed capital investment decisions.

His rigorous approach to evaluation ensures that the investment is not just financially sound. But also strategically aligned with the company's long-term goals. This example highlights the meticulous process of financial due diligence, stakeholder engagement, and strategic foresight that FP&A professionals bring to capital investment decisions.

Example 6: Navigating the Annual Budgeting Process

Elena, the Director of FP&A, leads her team through the annual budgeting process.

This year, they implemented a hybrid approach, combining top-down directives with bottom-up feedback to set financial targets and align budget allocations.

Initial Top-Down Guidance:

The process begins with the executive team. The execs include the CEO and CFO, setting overall corporate objectives and preliminary financial targets based on the company's strategic goals. Elena receives these top-down directives and is tasked with disseminating them across various departments.

Departmental Bottom-Up Submissions:

Elena distributes Excel budget templates. And instructs each department head to draft their initial budgets. These are based on their specific needs, projected costs, and planned initiatives for the upcoming year. Departments consider their personnel needs, operational costs, and development projects, aligning their proposals with the strategic priorities communicated by Elena.

Review and Consolidation:

Once departmental budgets are submitted. Elena's team consolidates them into a single preliminary budget. They review each department's requests in detail, checking for alignment with strategic priorities and assessing the realism of the proposed expenses and revenue forecasts.

Negotiation Meetings:

Elena facilitates a series of budget negotiation meetings. In these meetings discrepancies between the top-down targets and bottom-up submissions are addressed. They involve department heads and are aimed at reaching a consensus on budget targets and allocations. Elena encourages constructive dialogue, guiding the conversation to focus on strategic goals and the overall strategy of company.

Scenario Planning and Adjustments:

To accommodate various potential future states of the company and its market.

Elena's team develops multiple budget scenarios. These include optimistic, pessimistic, and most likely financial outcomes. This approach helps in understanding the impacts of different budgeting decisions under various economic conditions.

Finalisation and Approval:

After rigorous reviews, multiple back-and-forth and adjustments.

Elena and the team arrive at the final budget version, incorporating the agreed-upon changes from the negotiation meetings. This final version is presented to the executive team for approval.

Communication and Implementation:

Once approved, Elena oversees the communication of the final budget to the entire company. She explains department-specific allocations and budget guidance for the upcoming year. She also sets up a monitoring plan to track budget adherence throughout the year.

This example shows the collaborative nature of the annual budgeting process under Elena's leadership. It highlights how FP&A balances strategic goals with operational needs through careful planning, negotiation, and adjustment. This ensures the budget is not only a piece of document but a strategic tool that guides the company throughout the upcoming year.

Example 7: Digital Transformation and Automation:

Amelia is the VP of FP&A at a fast-growing tech company. She recognizes the need to enhance the department's technological capabilities to keep pace with the rapid growth and increasing complexities of the business

Amelia initiates and spearheads a digital transformation project. The project aimed at revolutionising how the FP&A functions operate.

Assessment of Current Technologies:

Amelia begins by conducting a thorough assessment of the existing systems and tools.

She identifies the limitations of current technologies, particularly in handling large datasets and generating real-time analytics. These are crucial for quick decision-making.

Selection of Advanced Financial Software:

After meeting different tool vendors and evaluating several options.

Amelia and the team decided to implement a system that integrates AI capabilities. The new tool once implemented will automate routine tasks, such as data entry and report generation. And provide sophisticated tools for predictive analytics and scenario planning. This will free up FP&A teams' time to focus on value-added business partnering.

Training and Change Management:

Understanding the challenges of adopting new technology. Amelia organises comprehensive training sessions for her team. These sessions are designed to familiarise everyone with the new system's functionalities and best practices. She also sets up a support system to address any issues as the team transitions to the new software.

Integration of AI and Data Analytics:

With the new system in place now. Amelia leads the integration of AI-driven tools that enhance financial forecasting. The AI algorithms analyse historical data to identify trends and patterns, enabling the FP&A team to make more accurate forecasts.

Pilot Testing and Rollout:

Before a full companywide rollout. Amelia initiates a pilot testing phase where selected SPOCs use the new tools to ensure they function as expected. Feedback from these tests is used to adjust and improve user experience.

Real-Time Reporting and Decision Support:

The new tool has real-time reporting capabilities. It significantly reduces the time it takes to generate financial reports and insights. Amelia and the team use these capabilities to provide executive leadership with timely data, supporting faster and more informed strategic decisions.

Evaluating Impact and Scaling:

After successful implementation and initial usage. Amelia and the team evaluate the impact of the project. They review improvements in efficiency, accuracy, and strategic impact. Based on these outcomes, the FP&A team plans a phased approach to expand the use of these technologies across the company.

This example demonstrates the critical role of FP&A in leading digital initiatives within a company.

Example 8: Strategizing Global Expansion

Carlos, the Head of FP&A at a consumer goods company, is tasked with leading the financial strategy for the company's expansion into a new international market.

His approach involves detailed planning and analysis to ensure the success of the new entry.

Market Analysis and Entry Strategy:

Carlos starts by collaborating with the market research team to gather insights. They investigate the economic, cultural, and regulatory landscapes of the target market.

Based on this information, he develops financial models that forecast potential revenues and costs associated with the new entry.

Currency Risk Management:

Understanding the complexities of operating in multiple currency environments.

Carlos implements a comprehensive currency risk management strategy. This includes the use of forward contracts and options to hedge against currency fluctuations.

He also sets up a monitoring system to regularly assess currency risks to adjust hedging strategies as needed.

Compliance with International Regulations:

To ensure compliance with international financial regulations. Carlos works closely with legal and compliance teams. He oversees the establishment of internal controls and procedures that adhere to local financial reporting standards, tax laws, and business regulations. This effort is crucial to avoid legal and financial penalties.

Local Financial Integration:

Carlos advises setting up a local finance team. They hire a local team member who is well-versed in regional business practices and can manage day-to-day finance operations. This new hire will play a critical role in customizing pricing strategies, managing local vendor relationships, and conducting regular oversight and analysis to align with the headquarters' expectations.

Training and Development:

Recognising the importance of having a well-informed team. Carlos arranges training sessions for both the central and local finance teams. These sessions cover key areas such as local financial practices, integration processes, and updates on international financial management strategies.

Regular Strategy Reviews:

Carlos establishes a routine of strategic review meetings that involve key stakeholders from the central and local teams.

These reviews help track the progress of the expansion, discuss challenges, and refine strategies as the market dynamics evolve. It ensures that the company remains agile and responsive to new opportunities and risks.

Long-term Financial Planning:

With the initial setup and operations underway. Carlos focuses on long-term financial planning to support sustained growth in the new market. This includes reinvestment strategies, capital allocation, and planning for potential expansions and acquisitions within the region.

In this example, Carlos and the team show us how FP&A play a pivotal role in global expansion strategies. FP&A helps ensure that the company not only enters new markets effectively. But also establishes a robust financial framework to support long-term success and compliance across borders.

Example 9: Integrating Sustainability (ESG factors) in Financial Planning

Nadia, the Director of FP&A at a leading manufacturing company, is tasked with spearheading the integration of sustainability initiatives into the company's financial strategy.

Her goal is to ensure that these initiatives not only contribute to environmental goals but also align with the company's long-term profitability.

Sustainability Audit and Strategic Planning:

Nadia starts by conducting a comprehensive sustainability audit in collaboration with the environmental affairs department.

This audit assesses current practices, identifies areas for improvement, and benchmarks against industry standards. Based on the findings, she develops a strategic plan for implementing sustainable practices that align with the company's core business objectives.

Financial Modelling of Green Investments:

Nadia and her team evaluate potential investments in green technology. These include energy-efficient systems, waste-reduction processes, and renewable energy sources.

They create detailed financial models to project the costs, savings, and payback periods of these investments. The models also factor in potential government incentives for sustainable practices.

ESG Factor Integration:

Understanding the importance of ESG factors, Nadia incorporates these into the company's financial evaluation criteria.

She develops metrics to assess the impact of sustainability initiatives on environmental outcomes, social responsibility, and governance standards.

These metrics help quantify the intangible benefits of these initiatives, such as improved brand reputation and customer loyalty.

Stakeholder Engagement and Reporting:

Nadia organizes workshops across the company to raise awareness about the importance of sustainability in financial planning. She also ensures that sustainability efforts are transparently reported in the company's annual financial reports and investor communications. Highlighting the alignment with ESG criteria and the expected impact on financial performance.

Performance Monitoring and Feedback Loop:

To measure the effectiveness of implemented initiatives. Nadia sets up a system for ongoing monitoring and reporting of sustainability metrics. This system tracks progress against environmental goals and financial targets, providing data-driven feedback that informs future adjustments.

Long-term Sustainability Roadmap:

With the initial strategies in place, Nadia plans for the long-term integration of sustainability into the company's business model. She outlines a roadmap for scaling up successful practices and exploring new areas where environmental damage impact can be further reduced without compromising financial viability.

In this example, Nadia and the team demonstrate how FP&A can make sustainability a core component of the company's strategy. Her approach ensures that environmental and social governance factors are not only included in company policy. But they are also part of the economic equation that drives profitability.

In this chapter, we explored a typical day in the life of FP&A teams.

Through various real-life scenarios, we've seen how FP&A professionals expertly navigate challenges, diligently support their company's strategic goals, and adaptively respond to ever-changing business needs.

The examples highlighted the essential skills and strategic insights that FP&A teams bring to the table. From crisis management and capital investment decisions to digital transformations and global expansion strategies.

FP&A professionals are not just number crunchers. They are strategic partners who ensure financial decisions strengthen operational capabilities and drive long-term growth. Their ability to integrate financial acumen with operational insights allows them to offer invaluable support in steering the company towards growth and sustainability.

As we move forward, In the next chapter will deep dive into the typical FP&A monthly calendar.

Chapter 6
The FP&A Monthly Calendar

Monthly Calendar

The FP&A calendar is a critical tool that helps finance professionals stay organised.

Why is it important to have an FP&A Calendar?

Effective FP&A requires a structured and disciplined approach to managing FP&A activities.

Having a well-defined calendar enables the team to anticipate upcoming tasks, plan ahead, and allocate resources effectively in order to optimise performance.

It also helps to track the tasks and plan for upcoming deadlines. This is where the FP&A Monthly Calendar comes in handy.

This chapter will detail the typical monthly activities in an FP&A calendar, highlighting the importance of each phase in the monthly cycle.

By understanding these regular tasks, FP&A teams and different stakeholders can ensure that they meet important deadlines.

Points to Remember before we get into the FP&A Calendar

1. FP&A Calendar is a Best Practice Calendar and Not Standard or a Rule

The FP&A monthly calendar presented in this chapter represents a compilation of best practices rather than strict rules.

It's important to understand that the specific activities and their timing can vary significantly. They depend on various factors such as the industry, the age and size of the company, and the maturity of the FP&A team.

This calendar serves as a guideline that can be adapted to fit the unique needs of different organisations.

Industry-wide Variations:

- **Technology Start-Up:** In a fast-paced tech start-up, the FP&A monthly calendar might focus more on cash flow management and rapid forecasting updates due to the high rate of change in the technology sector. The team might need weekly forecasting cycles to adjust to market dynamics quickly.

- **Manufacturing Firm:** For a mature manufacturing company, the FP&A calendar may emphasize cost analysis and efficiency metrics, with less frequent updates but deeper dives into variance analysis and capital expenditure planning due to the capital-intensive nature of the industry.

Company Age:

- **New Company:** A newly established company might not have established all formal processes. So, the FP&A calendar could be more fluid, focusing on establishing baseline financial systems, setting up initial budgeting processes, and managing start-up costs.
- **Established Company:** An older, more established company likely has a more structured FP&A calendar. That includes detailed and standardized processes for everything from reporting to analysis, reflecting the stability and predictability of their business operations.

FP&A Team Maturity:

- **Developing FP&A Team:** In a company where the FP&A function is still developing. The calendar might initially focus heavily on basic tasks such as managing the month-end close process and basic reporting. As the team matures, more sophisticated activities like ad hoc analysis and strategic advisory roles might gradually be integrated.
- **Mature FP&A Team:** A mature FP&A team in a large multinational might have a highly complex monthly calendar that integrates advanced analytics, detailed scenario planning, and strategic involvement in corporate decision-making, reflecting the team's advanced capabilities and strategic importance to the organisation.

2. Calendar Month Structure:

For clarity and simplicity, the calendar is organised by weeks within a typical month. For Example: Week 1 starts on Calendar Day 1 and ends on Calendar Day 7, and so forth.

This structure helps standardise the discussion around when tasks typically occur but should be adjusted according to the actual number of days in each month and specific business schedules.

Also, note we review prior month numbers in the current month calendar.

It is standard practice to review the financial numbers from the previous month during the current month.

For Example: If we are currently in the month of April, the FP&A team will be reviewing and analysing the financial results from March.

3. Exclusion of Annual Budgeting Process:

Note that the activities described in the FP&A monthly calendar exclude the annual budgeting process. Budgeting is a separate, comprehensive process that involves extensive planning and coordination and occurs once a year. The monthly calendar focuses instead on the recurring tasks that support the continuous financial management cycle every month.

To summarize Remember the FP&A Calendar ...

- Is best practice and not a rule or a standard and varies based on company size, industry, Age of the company and Age of the FP&A Team
- Talks about the previous month's numbers/performance.
- Doesn't talk about the budget.

Overview of the FP&A Monthly Calendar

Week 1	Week 2	Week 3	Week 4
• Flash Report (Rev , Exps) • Month close • Accounting Close Review • Month End reporting packs and BVA commentaries • Quarterly Reports	• Finance updates prelim forecast • Review forecast with business • Review forecast with BU head / CFO • Upload forecast in the system • Month End / Quarter End Reviews	• Recharges • WC Management • Special projects • Supporting business • Automation • Meeting business partners – Pulse Check – Risk & Opportunities	• Revenue flash / estimates • Revenue Close • AP close • Accruals / Prepaid JVs • Supporting business • Meeting business partners – Pulse Check – Risk & Opportunities

Week 1: Accounting Close and Management Reports

Begin with the accounting close process, which involves consolidating and finalising the financial data for the previous month. This phase includes generating flash reports and other key financial summaries that provide a snapshot of the company's financial health.

The preparation of management reports follows which are detailed documents that provide insights into financial performance, key metrics, and variances from the budget.

Week 2: Forecast Updates and Business Reviews

Update preliminary forecasts based on recent performance and any new business developments. This often involves revising financial projections and assumptions to reflect current market conditions and business realities.

Conduct business reviews with department heads to discuss the results, update forecasts, and gather feedback that will inform the next planning cycle.

Week 3: Special Projects and Strategic Initiatives

Focus on any special projects or strategic initiatives that require financial analysis and support. This could include profitability analysis, cost reduction initiatives, or investment appraisals.

This period may also involve preparing for any upcoming strategic meetings or presentations to the board or executive team.

Week 4: Preparation for the Month End and Week 1 of Next month.

The final week of the month is typically used to prepare for the upcoming month. This includes setting up tasks, aligning resources, and ensuring that the FP&A team is ready to handle the next month's activities efficiently.

In the remaining part of this chapter will provide a comprehensive look at the essential activities that comprise the FP&A monthly calendar.

Comprehensive Tasks Week Wise

WEEK 1: Accounting Close and Management Reports

Week 1	Week 2	Week 3	Week 4
• Flash Report (Rev , Exps) • Month close • Accounting Close Review • Month End reporting packs and BVA commentaries • Quarterly Reports	• Finance updates prelim forecast • Review forecast with business • Review forecast with BU head / CFO • Upload forecast in the system • Month End / Quarter End Reviews	• Recharges • WC Management • Special projects • Supporting business • Automation • Meeting business partners – Pulse Check – Risk & Opportunities	• Revenue flash / estimates • Revenue Close • AP close • Accruals / Prepaid JVs • Supporting business • Meeting business partners – Pulse Check – Risk & Opportunities

Flash Reports

Flash reports are summaries designed to provide a quick snapshot of a company's performance well before the detailed month-end reports are finalised.

These reports are crucial for senior management who need immediate insights to make timely decisions. Rather than waiting until all financial books are closed and comprehensive reports are ready by the end of Week 1 or later.

These reports serve as an early indicator of financial results and trends, enabling senior management to:

- **React Quickly:** They provide early warning signs of unexpected results, whether positive or negative, allowing management to respond promptly.
- **Make Timely Decisions:** Flash reports help executives make informed decisions rapidly, without waiting for the full details that come later in the financial cycle.
- **Monitor Vital Metrics:** They focus on key financial metrics such as revenue, expenses, and cash flow, offering a quick health check on these critical areas.

Key Characteristics of Flash Reporting:

- **Speed:** Flash reports are prepared very quickly after a period ends, often within the first few days of the month.

- **Simplicity:** They typically include only the most critical financial data, avoiding the complexity of full financial statements.
- **Frequency:** Because they are designed to be prepared and distributed quickly, they can be issued more frequently, often weekly, or sometimes even daily, depending on the company's needs.

Example: A retail company starts a big sale in the middle of a month. Management could use a flash report to quickly see the initial impact of the sale on revenue and profits, without waiting for the detailed monthly reports. This early data allows them to adjust marketing strategies or inventory orders based on actual sales performance.

In summary,

- Flash reports act as a high-level, early glimpse providing essential data to senior management at a speed that matches the pace of decision-making:
- They are a Brief summary of financial data and key performance indicators (KPIs) that provide a snapshot of a company's financial health and performance.
- They cover a specific period, a day, week, or month, and are prepared quickly to provide timely insights.
- Focuses on the most critical information and highlights any significant changes or trends.
- A way to keep decision-makers updated on the financial performance and enable them to make informed decisions based on the current state of the business.
- They bridge the gap between month-end reports.

Month Close and Accounting Reviews

- Month close is a process that ensures that all financial transactions for that period are recorded accurately and completely.
- FP&A assists the accounting team in a smooth month-end close.
- BVA stands for Budget Variance Analysis and helps assess how well the company's actual financial results align with the budgeted expectations.

- It involves comparing the budgeted revenues, expenses, and other financial metrics with the actual figures and analysing the variances.
- Focuses on the most critical information and highlights any significant changes or trends.

Month End Reporting Packs with Commentaries

- Detailed overview of the company's financial performance, key metrics, and other relevant information for that month.
- Typically distributed to senior management, to keep them informed about the financial health of the organisation.
- Here the actual results from last month are compared to both the budget and the most up-to-date forecast.
- It contains variance analysis, business commentary and recommendations.

Here is a snapshot from a company's month-end reporting slide:

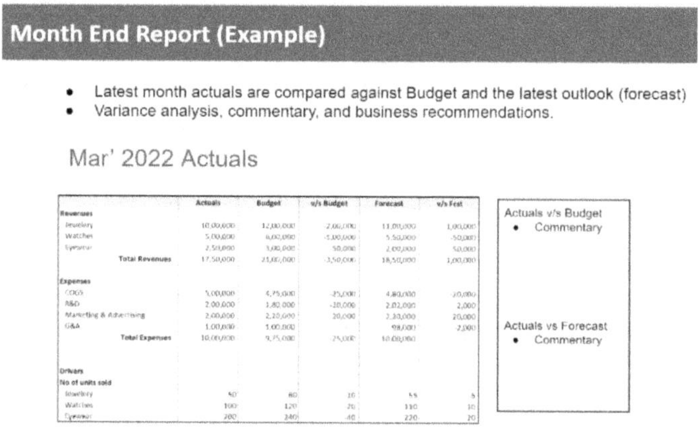

Quarter End Reports / Quarterly Business Review Deck:

- Discusses Highlights, Lowlights and Key Learnings from the previous quarter.
- Provide a detailed overview of Significant Risks, Opportunities, Action Plans, OKRs or Targets and Forecast for the next quarter.

- Identifies adjustments that need to be made in the next quarter based on previous quarters' performance.

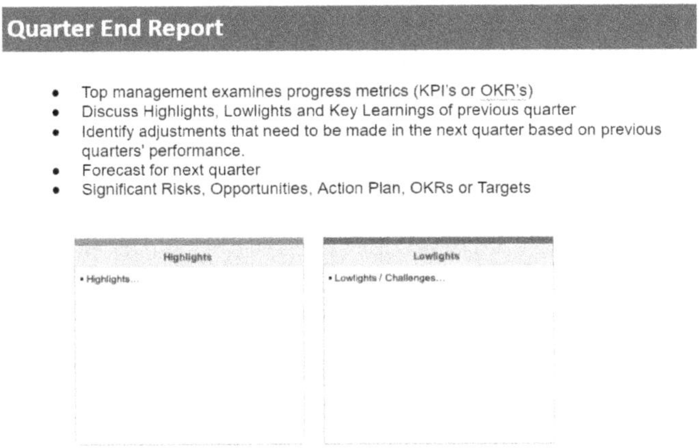

To summarize during the first week, FP&A focus lies on Accounting Close and Management Reports. It covers Flash reports, month close and accounting reviews, month-end reporting packs with commentaries, and quarter-end reports.

Next let's move to Week 2 ...

WEEK 2: Forecasting

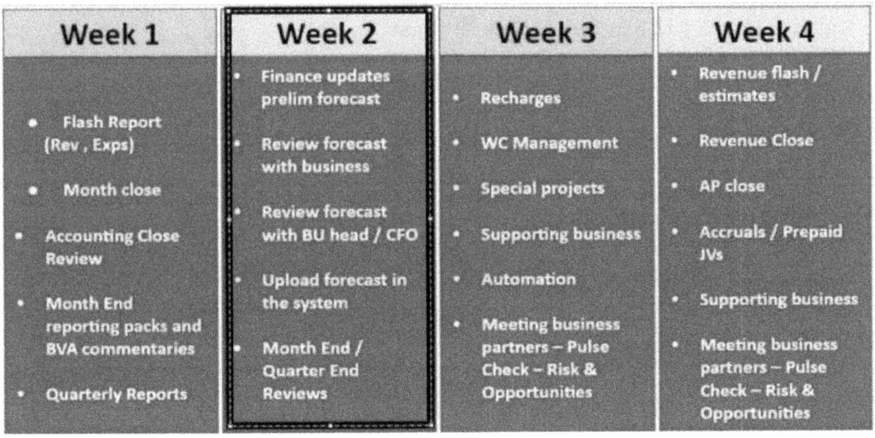

Week 2 is All about Forecasting. Here are the 5 steps:

Step 1. FP&A updates prelim Forecast.

The Forecast cycle starts with FP&A reviewing historical performance, assessing current trends, and considering any external factors that may impact the forecast.

The FP&A team incorporates this information into the preliminary forecast.

Step 2. FP&A Reviews forecast with business teams.

Collaboration with key business teams is vital for accurate forecasting.

The FP&A team engages with department heads, sales teams, marketing teams, and other relevant stakeholders to gather their inputs and insights.

This collaborative effort ensures that the forecast aligns with the operational realities of the business.

The FP&A team incorporates feedback from these teams and refines the forecast accordingly.

Step 3. FP&A Reviews forecast with CFO.

The FP&A team presents the forecast, discusses key assumptions, and seeks input from the CFO.

The CFO provides valuable insights, challenges assumptions, and ensures the forecast is in line with the organisation's financial goals and objectives.

Step 4. Upload + LOCK forecast in the system.

Once the forecast is finalised, it is uploaded into the designated financial planning system.

Uploading the forecast into a centralised system facilitates easy access, data consolidation, and automated reporting.

To maintain consistency and integrity, it is crucial to lock the current forecast once it has been uploaded into the system.

This ensures that the forecast remains unchanged, preventing inadvertent modifications that could compromise accuracy.

Locking in the forecast also establishes a clear baseline for tracking performance and enables effective comparison with actual results.

Month-end / Quarter end business reviews (MBR's and QBR's)

These meetings bring together FP&A and business stakeholders to review the financial performance, discuss variances, and gain insights into the factors driving the results.

Month-end reviews involve analysing the financial results for a specific month, including revenue, expenses, and other key financial metrics.

Quarter-end reviews are more comprehensive and encompass the entire three-month period.

Week 3: A Time for Strategic Focus and Preparation

Week 3 stands out as a period that typically carries a lighter workload compared to the intense activities in Weeks 1, 2, and 4.

It provides a valuable opportunity for the FP&A team to:

- **Plan for Leaves:** Given the less demanding nature of this week, team members often find it an ideal time to schedule leaves. This planning ensures that the team remains well-rested and effective, particularly important in managing the more intense demands of the closing and reporting periods.

- **Focus on Special Projects:** With the routine financial tasks under less pressure, Week 3 is an excellent time for the FP&A team to dive into special projects. These projects might include strategic initiatives, such as exploring new investment opportunities, conducting detailed profitability analysis, or developing new financial models that will drive future growth.

- **Advance Automation Efforts:** Leveraging the relatively quieter period, efforts to enhance efficiency through automation can be prioritised. This could involve upgrading financial software, streamlining data collection processes, or implementing new tools that reduce manual effort and improve accuracy.

- **Preparation for Next Month:** Week 3 also allows the team to begin preparations for the upcoming month. This includes setting up frameworks for the next cycle of reporting, forecasting, and analysis, ensuring that the team is well-prepared to handle the forthcoming tasks efficiently.

By using Week 3 strategically, FP&A teams can ensure that they not only maintain ongoing operations smoothly but also enhance their strategic capabilities and readiness for future challenges.

Here are some common tasks during this period:

1. Recharges and Allocations

Recharges involve transferring costs incurred by one department or entity to another within the same organisation.

Allocations are used to distribute costs across different departments or cost centres based on predefined allocation methods. A way of assigning shared costs to various entities or business units based on predetermined criteria, such as the proportion of usage, headcount, revenue, etc.

Both recharges and allocations are important tools for accurately assigning costs within an organisation, enabling better cost visibility and accountability.

2. Profitability Analysis

Provides insights into the most profitable aspects of the business and guides decision-making to maximize profitability.

Examples: BU wise Profitability, Branch Profitability, Customer wise Profitability, Project wise Profitability, Country wise Profitability etc.

3. Working Capital Management

Monitor and optimise the company's short-term liquidity and operational efficiency If there is no separate treasury team.

Ensure that the company has enough cash and resources to support its day-to-day operations while minimising unnecessary costs tied up in working capital.

Activities: Cashflow Forecasting, Working Capital Efficiency initiatives etc.

4. Automation:

By automating repetitive tasks, improving data accuracy, and enabling efficient analysis and by embracing automation, FP&A teams can focus more on value-added activities and provide timely insights to drive strategic decision-making.

5. Special Projects and Supporting the Business:

FP&A plays a vital role in special cross-functional projects by providing financial analysis, budgeting, forecasting, and decision support.

Their involvement ensures that projects are financially viable, align with strategic goals, and are effectively managed from a financial perspective throughout their lifecycle.

6. Risk and Opportunities Assessment:

By actively assessing risks and opportunities, FP&A helps organisations make informed decisions to mitigate risks, exploit opportunities, and improve financial performance.

WEEK 4: Month end Close & Preparation for Week 1

1. Flash Reports (Revenues/Expenses)

- Flash reporting, which we saw at the beginning of Week 1 earlier in this chapter typically starts at the end of the month, even before the actual financial data for that period is fully available.
- They contain preliminary data that offer an initial evaluation of financial performance.
- They serve as a foundation for further analysis and reporting when the actual data is accessible.

2. Revenue Close.

Revenue close is the process of finalising and accurately recording revenue-related transactions and activities within an organisation.

FP&A collaborates with the accounting department to validate the accuracy and completeness of revenue-related data.

3. Accounts Payable Close, Accruals, Prepaid JVs.

FP&A assists in the process of identifying and calculating accruals for expenses that are applicable to the current accounting period but have not yet been billed or paid.

Prepaid expenses are advance payments made by a company for goods or services that will be utilised in the future. FP&A assists accounting in accurately recording and managing these prepayments.

This chapter has systematically explored the FP&A monthly calendar.

A fundamental framework that guides the activities of FP&A teams.

Each week of the calendar is meticulously planned to ensure comprehensive management of tasks—from the closing of books and preparation of management reports to strategic reviews and preparation for upcoming challenges.

We began with Week 1 where the focus is on closing the previous month's accounts and generating initial financial reports.

This sets the stage for Week 2, which involves deep dives into financial forecasting and performance reviews, essential for adjusting strategies in real-time.

Week 3 offers a lighter schedule, allowing teams to focus on special projects, automation enhancements, and strategic planning without the pressure of immediate deadlines.

Finally, Week 4 wraps up the month with preparations for the next cycle, ensuring a smooth transition and readiness for new challenges.

Quick Recap of the FP&A Calendar

- Week 1: Accounting Close and Management Reporting
- Week 2: Forecasting and Business Reviews.
- Week 3: Other Items, Special Projects & Automation
- Week 4: Month-end Close & Preparation for Week

As we conclude this chapter, it is clear that the FP&A monthly calendar is not just a schedule but a strategic tool that enables FP&A teams to operate efficiently.

The insights garnered here will serve as a foundation for your FP&A career.

Preparation is key in FP&A. Up next; we will discuss how you can prepare effectively for your first or the next FP&A role.

Section 3

Preparing For The FP&A Role

Chapter 7

FP&A Resume Blueprint

Your First Impression

Your resume is your opportunity to make a favourable first impression.

In FP&A roles where precision is important. How you construct your resume can speak volumes about your capabilities.

In this chapter, we dive into each component of the resume. From the key objective and goals to the intricacies of bullet points.

Additionally, we'll explore common pitfalls in resume writing and how to avoid them.

The chapter concludes with advanced LinkedIn optimisation strategies. These insights will help you enhance your online presence, making your profile more attractive to recruiters and aligning it with your career aspirations in FP&A.

So, let's start and make sure every element of your resume presents a compelling narrative of your professional journey.

I thought it would be best if I use my resume to teach and show you these steps.

So, here is my resume which we will use to understand the different parts of a Resume.

ASIF MASANI

asif@fpnaprofessionals.com   https://www.linkedin.com/in/asifmasani   +91 8097379663

1. **Your Name and Contact Information.**

- Your name is presented in a larger, bold font, making it immediately noticeable. This ensures that your name stands out as the most prominent element, which is standard practice for resumes.

- Contact Information: The email address, LinkedIn profile, and phone number are listed alongside the name but in a smaller font. This placement allows for easy identification.

ASIF MASANI

asif@fpnaprofessionals.com https://www.linkedin.com/in/asifmasani +91 8097379663

FP&A PROFESSIONAL SUMMARY

- FP&A Professional with 13+ Years of Finance and FP&A experience working with EY, Citi, Coursera
- Recognized among the world's Top 20 FP&A professional in 2022, 2023 and 2024
- Built a community of 140,000+ FP&A Professionals on LinkedIn
- Author of the Amazon bestselling book "All About FP&A" (#14 bestseller in Management Accounting category)

PROFESSIONAL EXPERIENCE

FP&A Professionals Institute (FPI) Mumbai, India
Co- Founder & Lead Faculty *November 2023 - Present*

- Co-Founder of FP&A Professionals Institute (FPI) with a mission to upskill 1 million finance professionals in FP&A.
- My blog articles have been featured on FP&A trends, Finance Alliance, FP&A Professionals & more
- Recognized among the world's Top 20 FP&A professional in 2022, 2023 and 2024
- Coached and Trained 1K+ finance professionals via my Live and self-paced FP&A Courses

Coursera Mumbai, India
FP&A Lead, APAC India *June 2021- Jan 2024*

- Drove Budgets & Forecasts for Coursera's Consumer APAC Businesses. (Revenue budget ~$100M)
- Lead Month end (MER's) and Quarter end business reviews (QBR's) for the region.
- Lead cross functional initiatives working closely with Sales, Marketing, Operations and Product teams

Great Learning Mumbai, India
Sr. Manager FP&A *November 2020 - June 2021*

- Crafting management reports and Analysis on Sales, Marketing and Operations ($100M+ Business)
- Due Diligence and investor reporting (for acquisition).

Citi Bank Mumbai, India
FP&A Manager *April 2014 - April 2019*

- Reporting key business drivers for Citi's Retail Bank and Credit Cards for management reviews.
- Managed a P&L of ~$2Bn and Expense Budget of ~$500Mn. Won 2 awards: Employee of the month and Extra miler

EY Mumbai, India
Executive, Audit *April 2010 - Dec 2013*

- Responsible for planning, executing, and concluding statutory and tax audits within specific deadlines.
- Audited listed Indian companies including ITD Cementation, Gammon, India bulls and Bharat Hotels.

EDUCATION

Institute of Chartered Accountants of India
Chartered Accountant, India *April 2008 – Nov 2012*

Bachelor of Commerce in Accounting and Finance
Narsee Monjee College, Mumbai University *April 2008 -Mar 2011*

INTERESTS

- Writing (Author of All About FP&A, currently writing 2 books: Accounting to FP&A and Crafting Visual Stories from Data, I write daily posts on Linkedin to 140K Followers and a weekly newsletter to 30K subscribers)
- Video Editing (Created 50+ FP&A Learning Videos on YouTube with 6K subscribers)
- Graphic Design (Created 100+ Infographics on FP&A on Linkedin)
- Watching Movies and Cricket (If I'm not writing, teaching, and editing videos you will find me in a movie theatre or a cricket stadium)

- I prefer to avoid adding the address. This is because usually address does not add any value. Also, it might restrict your chances if the screening criteria have a location preference.

2. Professional Summary / Key Objective

FP&A PROFESSIONAL SUMMARY

- FP&A Professional with 13+ Years of Finance and FP&A experience working with EY, Citi, Coursera
- Recognized among the world's Top 20 FP&A professional in 2022, 2023 and 2024
- Built a community of 140,000+ FP&A Professionals on LinkedIn
- Author of the Amazon bestselling book "All About FP&A" (#14 bestseller in Management Accounting category)

- Here you can make a strong and immediate impression. The goal is to capture the recruiter's attention and encourage them to read on.
- It's a concise statement that highlights your professional identity, key skills, and the value you can bring to an FP&A role.

A common mistake I see in crafting professional summaries is the use of vague statements. This does not provide clear, quantifiable evidence of a candidate's skills and achievements. Such statements can fail to convey the specific value the candidate brings to the table.

For example:

"Experienced FP&A professional with a strong background in finance and a track record of success." Or

"Looking for a challenging FP&A role where I can utilise my skills and experience to drive company growth." Or

"A finance professional seeking to leverage extensive industry knowledge in a dynamic financial environment." Or

"Motivated individual looking to advance my career in a forward-thinking company that values innovation and hard work."

Why these don't work:

- The statement is broad and doesn't offer any measurable metrics or specific experiences that demonstrate the candidate's qualifications.
- Terms like "strong background", "motivated individual" and "track record of success" are generic and can be applied to almost any candidate. This makes it difficult to stand out.
- These statements don't differentiate you from others who may have similar backgrounds.

Better Way: How to write an impactful professional summary?

"FP&A Lead with over 14 years of experience, including direct responsibility for managing a $500Mn expense budget at Citi Bank. Increased forecasting accuracy by 10% through advanced analytics at Coursera and recognised as a Top 20 FP&A Professional globally for three consecutive years."

Why does this version work?

- It provides specific facts and accomplishments, like managing a significant portfolio size and improving forecasting accuracy.
- The inclusion of the Top 20 recognition offers a unique talking point that sets the candidate apart from others.
- The statement offers clear, verifiable claims that can be discussed in more detail during the interview, providing substance for conversation.

Here are some more examples:

"Seasoned Auditor with 5+ years of experience, recognised for making process improvements that enhanced reporting accuracy by 25%, seeking to leverage my analytical skills for strategic impact in an FP&A capacity."

PROFESSIONAL EXPERIENCE

FP&A Professionals Institute (FPI) Mumbai, India
Co- Founder & Lead Faculty *November 2023 - Present*
- Co-Founder of FP&A Professionals Institute (FPI) with a mission to upskill 1 million finance professionals in FP&A.
- My blog articles have been featured on FP&A trends, Finance Alliance, FP&A Professionals & more
- Recognized among the world's Top 20 FP&A professional in 2022, 2023 and 2024
- Coached and Trained 1K+ finance professionals via my Live and self-paced FP&A Courses

Coursera Mumbai, India
FP&A Lead, APAC India *June 2021- Jan 2024*
- Drove Budgets & Forecasts for Coursera's Consumer APAC Businesses. (Revenue budget ~$100M)
- Lead Month end (MER's) and Quarter end business reviews (QBR's) for the region.
- Lead cross functional initiatives working closely with Sales, Marketing, Operations and Product teams

Great Learning Mumbai, India
Sr. Manager FP&A *November 2020 - June 2021*
- Crafting management reports and Analysis on Sales, Marketing and Operations ($100M+ Business)
- Due Diligence and investor reporting (for acquisition).

Citi Bank Mumbai, India
FP&A Manager *April 2014 - April 2019*
- Reporting key business drivers for Citi's Retail Bank and Credit Cards for management reviews.
- Managed a P&L of ~$2Bn and Expense Budget of ~$500Mn. Won 2 awards: Employee of the month and Extra miler

EY Mumbai, India
Executive, Audit *April 2010 - Dec 2013*
- Responsible for planning, executing, and concluding statutory and tax audits within specific deadlines.
- Audited listed Indian companies including ITD Cementation, Gammon, India bulls and Bharat Hotels.

"Accountant with 3 years' experience. Cut month-end close time by 40%, seeking to apply my analysis skills in an FP&A role."

"Analyst with 2 years' experience. Improved forecast accuracy by 20%, eager to leverage my experience in an FP&A position."

3. **Work or Professional Experience Section:**

Here's how you can structure the Work Experience section on your resume.

Best Practices and Mistakes to Avoid

1. **Highlight Results, Not Just Duties:**

- Resumes fall short by merely summarising job duties. Instead emphasise the results or impact of those duties.
- To differentiate yourself, focus each bullet point on the outcomes of your actions. And quantify the impact whenever possible.
- For example, instead of saying "Managed budget and forecast," specify "Managed an expense budget of $500 Mn and improved forecast accuracy by 10% within six months."

2. **Avoid Common Mistakes:**

- Do not get overly caught up in the aesthetics of your resume.
- For example, don't look for fancy templates or fonts, at the expense of substantive, impactful content.
- It's important to focus on clear, concise, and result-driven bullet points that communicate your value effectively.

3. **Sell Your Experience:**

- Shift from a task-based description to a value-based description.
- Sell your experience by articulating how the tasks you performed led to meaningful contributions.
- For example, if you worked in FP&A, instead of "Prepared reports," you might write, "Streamlined reporting processes, reducing report preparation time by 30 % enhancing decision-making across the company."

4. Customize for the Role:

- Tailor your work experience to reflect the skills and experiences most relevant to the FP&A role you are targeting.
- Highlight experiences that demonstrates key FP&A competencies like analytical thinking, financial forecasting, and strategic planning.

5. Structure and Clarity:

- Keep your descriptions concise but informative.
- Each role should be well-defined with clear bullet points that describe not only what you did but how well you did it and the effect it had.
- Limit the number of bullet points to maintain clarity and impact, ideally no more than three to five per role.

6. Use of Keywords:

- Integrate relevant keywords throughout your work experience section.
- These ***keywords should align with those used in the job description*** to ensure your resume passes through Applicant Tracking Systems (ATS) and catches the eye of hiring managers.

7. Formatting:

- Start with the most recent position and work backwards.
- Use a clear, easy-to-read format with your job title, the company's name and the dates of employment prominently displayed.

8. Quantifiable Achievements:

- Where possible, quantify your achievements with numbers, percentages, or specific milestones to provide concrete evidence of your capabilities and impact.

9. Active Language:

- Use active verbs to describe your job responsibilities and achievements, such as "implemented," "transformed," "achieved," etc.

- This not only makes your resume is more dynamic but also shows your direct involvement and impact in your roles.

Example 1:

Here is how you might list a job in the Work Experience section:

Senior Financial Analyst | XYZ Corporation | May 2016 – Present

- Spearheaded a budget overhaul that cut costs by 20% within the first year.
- Developed a financial modelling tool that improved forecasting accuracy by 35%.
- Led a cross-departmental team to streamline the quarterly financial reporting process, reducing time spent by 25% and increasing report accuracy.

Example 2: For someone in Audit who wishes to move to FP&A

Senior Auditor | ABC Audit Firm | January 2018 - Present

- Identified and addressed risks preventing potential losses of $100K+ annually for client XYZ.
- Lead automation project that led to a 15% improvement in reporting accuracy for client ABC.
- Spearheaded a project to automate parts of the internal audit process using SQL, reducing the audit cycle time by 20% and enhancing accuracy.

Example 3: For someone in accounting who wishes to move to FP&A

Corporate Accountant | JKL Energy Solutions | October 2011 - December 2013

- Oversaw capital budgeting process to guide decisions on $50M Investment.
- Developed dashboards to track KPIs in real time saving 200+ hours annually on manual reporting and facilitating quicker decision making.
- Trained a team of 30 Junior accountants on best practices replicating the same in different departments adding efficiency gains of 1000+ hours annually.

By focusing on these elements, you'll craft a work experience section that not only details what you've done. But more importantly, showcases your contributions and the tangible value you've brought to your past roles.

4. Education Section

EDUCATION

Institute of Chartered Accountants of India
Chartered Accountant, India *April 2008 – Nov 2012*

Bachelor of Commerce in Accounting and Finance
Narsee Monjee College, Mumbai University *April 2008 -Mar 2011*

We will not spend a lot of time here as this section is relatively straightforward.

Here are a few quick tips:

- It should highlight degrees, certifications, and training that are relevant to FP&A roles. List your highest degree first. Include the degree/certification, the name of the institution, and the graduation year.

- If you have taken recent courses highly the ones relevant to the FP&A role. Example: Certificate on Financial Modelling for FP&A or Certified Global FP&A Certification (CGFPA) or FP&A Masterclass etc.

5. Interest / Hobbies Section

INTERESTS

- Writing (Author of All About FP&A, currently writing 2 books: Accounting to FP&A and Crafting Visual Stories from Data, I write daily posts on Linkedin to 140K Followers and a weekly newsletter to 30K subscribers)
- Video Editing (Created 50+ FP&A Learning Videos on YouTube with 6K subscribers)
- Graphic Design (Created 100+ Infographics on FP&A on Linkedin)
- Watching Movies and Cricket (If I'm not writing, teaching, and editing videos you will find me in a movie theatre or a cricket stadium)

The Interests section of your resume, while often overlooked, plays a crucial role in humanising your application. It provides a fuller picture of who you are beyond your professional and academic qualifications.

Most importantly it can be a conversation starter and a way to connect with the interviewer on a more personal level.

Here are Quick tips:

- Shows that you have a balanced life, engaging in activities that enhance your personal growth and skills that are often transferable to the workplace.

- Gives employers a glimpse into your personality, which can help them assess whether you'd be a good cultural fit within their team or company culture.
- Certain hobbies or interests can highlight unique skills that are not evident from your work experience or education sections. But can be valuable in the workplace, such as teamwork, leadership, or creativity.
- Only include interests that are a true reflection of your personality and activities. Authenticity matters because it might come up in an interview, and you should be able to discuss your interests passionately and genuinely.
- While it's a more personal section, maintain professionalism. Avoid controversial hobbies that could be troublesome like politics, religion etc. Stick to interests that either enhance your professional image or demonstrate transferable skills.
- Whenever possible, relate your interests to skills that are pertinent to the job. For example, if you are applying for an FP&A role that requires meticulous attention to detail, you might mention hobbies like model building or intricate crafting.
- This section should not overshadow more critical sections like your experience or skills. A few concise lines or bullet points are sufficient.
- Anything you list should be something you are comfortable with and prepared to discuss in an interview. Sometimes, interests can serve as a pleasant icebreaker or a way to lighten the conversation.

Crafting an effective FP&A resume requires attention to detail, careful structuring, and personalisation to showcase your unique qualifications and experiences. Remember, each part of the resume must work cohesively to highlight your readiness for FP&A roles.

5 Common Resume Mistakes and How You Can Avoid Them:

1. **Focusing on Duties Rather Than Achievements**

   - **Mistake:** Resumes often list job duties instead of focusing on achievements.

- **Pro Tip:** Emphasize specific achievements and quantify the impact of your actions to demonstrate effectiveness.

2. **Overusing Buzzwords and Clichés:**

- **Mistake:** Frequent use of generic buzzwords and clichés dilutes the impact of your resume.
- **Pro Tip:** Use precise, tangible language to describe your accomplishments and avoid vague terms.

3. **Ignoring the Needs of the Employer:**

- **Mistake:** Failing to tailor your resume to the specific needs of the employer.
- **Pro Tip:** Customize your resume for each application by incorporating relevant keywords and focusing on experiences that match the job requirements.

4. Neglecting the Appearance and Readability:

- **Mistake:** Using complex layouts that compromise the readability and ATS compatibility of your resume.
- **Pro Tip:** Opt for a simple, professional layout with standard fonts and clear headings, ensuring the format is ATS-friendly.

5. Excessive Length:

- **Mistake:** Creating a resume that is too long potentially loses the reader's interest.
- **Pro Tip:** Keep your resume concise, ideally to one or two pages (one page is best) Include only relevant information.

Optimising Your LinkedIn Profile for FP&A Roles

Think of your LinkedIn profile as your digital landing page rather than just a virtual resume.

Effective LinkedIn SEO (Search Engine Optimization) is crucial for enhancing your visibility among recruiters searching for top FP&A talent.

By fine-tuning your profile, you help LinkedIn's algorithms better understand and elevate your profile in search results. This can significantly boost your chances of being noticed for relevant FP&A opportunities by recruiters and hiring managers on Linkedin.

Here are 20 touchpoints to focus on for optimising your LinkedIn profile:

1. **Experience Section:** Incorporate FP&A-specific keywords such as 'budgeting,' 'forecasting,' and 'strategic analysis' to enhance relevance.
2. **Education Section:** List any degrees and include FP&A-related courses or certifications to underscore your expertise.
3. **Banner:** Ensure your banner visually aligns with your professional focus in FP&A.
4. **Endorsements:** Actively seek endorsements for FP&A relevant skills from colleagues.
5. **Profile Headline:** Use strategic keywords like 'FP&A Specialist' to improve discoverability.
6. **Profile Photo:** Display a professional headshot that conveys credibility.
7. **Summary Section:** Articulate your experience and skills in FP&A, highlighting major achievements and capabilities.
8. **Skills Section:** Add and priortise FP&A-related skills such as 'financial modelling,' 'data analysis,' etc.
9. **Recommendations:** Request recommendations from past colleagues or managers who can attest to your FP&A skills.
10. **Featured Content:** Highlight key posts, projects, or documents that showcase your expertise in FP&A.
11. **Volunteer Experience:** Include any volunteer roles where you applied or developed transferable FP&A skills.
12. **Certifications:** List any certifications directly relevant to FP&A like CFA, CPA, or FP&A certification.
13. **Accomplishments:** Mention awards, other recognitions, or key achievements relevant to your FP&A career.

14. **Location:** Ensure your location is updated to reflect where you are professionally based or seeking opportunities.

15. **Interests and Groups:** Join and participate in LinkedIn groups related to FP&A and finance.

16. **External Blog Articles:** Write and share a few articles on topics pertinent to FP&A and share them on Linkedin demonstrating thought leadership.

17. **Honors and Awards:** Include any honours that highlights your professional standing in the finance community.

18. **Linkedin Long Articles:** Publish detailed articles on LinkedIn FP&A topics that can attract views and show your depth of knowledge.

19. **Open to Work:** If job searching, use the 'Open to Work' feature to signal to recruiters but consider setting it to visible to recruiters only.

20. **LinkedIn Premium:** Consider subscribing to LinkedIn Premium while job hunting to access additional features that can aid your search.

By carefully addressing these touchpoints, your LinkedIn profile will not only reflect your FP&A expertise but also improve your visibility in recruiter searches.

A well-optimized LinkedIn profile can be a game-changer in your job search.

In this chapter, we saw in detail how to craft each section of your FP&A resume.

- From articulating a compelling professional summary to detailing impactful work experiences and optimising your LinkedIn profile.

- Whether refining bullet points or tailoring your digital presence, the principles laid out in this chapter can serve as your blueprint for success in securing your next FP&A role.

By applying these strategies, you can position yourself as a standout candidate who not only meets but exceeds the requirements of top-tier FP&A positions. With your resume in hand, let's get you ready to ace the FP&A interview.

Chapter 8

FP&A Interview Prep Secrets

Interview Preparation Guide for FP&A Roles

Securing a role in FP&A demands more than just a solid grasp of FP&A fundamentals.

It requires a strategic approach to nailing the Interview process.

In this chapter, we will:

1. First, we look at what interviewers typically look for in ideal FP&A candidates. These are qualities that go beyond technical FP&A and excel in knowledge.
2. Next, streamline your preparation and remove guesswork. Here, we introduce the FP&A Interview Prep Secret Framework. This is a structured approach that will Provide a proven checklist that guides you through each step of the interview process.
3. Finally, we will look at practical tips and real-life advice from seasoned FP&A professionals to handle common interview challenges.

By the end of this chapter, you will be equipped to not only face FP&A interviews with confidence but also stand out as a candidate perfectly suited for your next FP&A role.

4 Key Traits Interviewers Seek in Top Candidates

Today the Interviewers are looking for much more than number crunchers.

They want professionals who will bring not only analytical skills. Along with hard skills, soft skills are necessary to inspire teams, drive innovation, and align with broader business objectives.

By demonstrating these qualities, candidates can noticeably increase their chances of securing a FP&A job.

Here are 4 Key Qualities FP&A Interviewers Seek in Top Candidates

1. **Positive Attitude and High Energy:**

Interviewers look for candidates who demonstrate a positive attitude and high energy. Candidates with a proactive attitude are perceived as more adaptable. And capable of navigating the ups and downs which is a big part of the FP&A role.

A candidate's attitude during an interview can reveal their potential to:

- **Handle Stress:** FP&A roles can be stressful, given tight deadlines and critical financial implications. A positive attitude helps in managing stress constructively without letting it impact the quality of work or team morale.
- **Foster Collaboration:** FP&A professionals often work in cross-functional teams. A collaborative attitude facilitates effective communication and teamwork across departments.
- **Drive Change:** Candidates who show a positive and open-minded attitude are perceived more likely to drive and adapt to change.

So, show high energy and excitement about the opportunity to grow and contribute to the role. Energy sums up a candidate's proactive engagement. This attribute is highly valued by interviewers as it directly influences not only individual performance but also the overall productivity and morale of the FP&A team.

How to convey High Energy in Interviews:

To effectively communicate high energy during an interview, candidates can:

- **Speak a little louder** than usual. Imagine you have a TV remote, and you have to up your volume by 1-2 points.
- **Tell Stories.** Share specific examples where your energy was a key factor in overcoming significant challenges or achieving team goals.
- **Demonstrate Enthusiasm for Learning and Growth.** Express a strong desire for continual learning and professional development.
- Use a **vibrant tone** and **active body language**.
- **Be articulate and expressive** during the interview.

2. **Enthusiasm:**

Enthusiasm and curiosity about the role are telling signs of a candidate who will continue to grow and contribute to the organisation.

Enthusiasm in a candidate indicates:

- Candidates passionate about their roles are more likely to stay long-term, reducing turnover and building stability within the FP&A team.
- Enthusiasm is often paired with a curiosity that drives continuous learning and professional development.
- Enthusiastic candidates are more likely to take initiative, seek out new projects, and go beyond the requirements of their job to add value.

How to show Enthusiasm in Interviews?

- **Provide specific instances** from past roles where your enthusiasm led to measurable achievements.
- **Tell stories** that reflect passion for FP&A or the industry, highlighting personal involvement in projects that had significant impact.
- **Ask good questions** and engage actively with the interviewer. Show a keen interest in the company. And don't forget to express how you can contribute to their success.

3. **Cultural Fit:**

Every company has its unique culture and values.

And ensuring that a candidate can thrive within that culture is becoming important. Cultural fit is about more than just getting along with colleagues. It's about sharing the core values and visions of the company.

Make sure you know very well the mission, vision, and the core values of the company. This can easily be found on the company's website.

Identify common values and bring out in your conversation any past experience of the shared common values.

4. **Initiative and Curiosity:**

The initiative is about taking charge, creating opportunities, and demonstrating leadership without being prompted. It shows that you are self-motivated and eager to bring positive changes or improvements.

The ability to anticipate needs and take independent action is a key trait. Demonstrating initiative, therefore, is highly valued.

Here's how to effectively communicate these attributes:

Provide stories from your previous experiences where you identified a problem, proposed a solution, and took the lead on implementing it.

For instance, talk about a time when you introduced a new financial tool or process that increased efficiency or reduced errors in your department.

Discuss any projects or tasks where you went beyond your regular duties to achieve something significant.

For example, if you volunteered to tackle a challenging project when others were hesitant. Or if you took the initiative to get additional training that was beneficial for your team.

Mention any instances where your proactive thinking helped avert a crisis or significantly benefited your company.

Curiosity

Curiosity is your eagerness to learn, understand deeper aspects and continuously improve your skills. It indicates a growth mindset, which is highly valuable in FP&A.

Talk about your continuous learning efforts, such as pursuing relevant certifications, attending workshops, or participating in industry seminars.

Mention how these activities have enriched your professional abilities and how you apply the acquired knowledge in practical scenarios.

Prepare thoughtful, informed questions for the interviewer about the company's financial strategies, challenges, or any recent financial news relevant to the company. This demonstrates not only your knowledge of the industry but also your interest in how the company operates and succeeds.

Mention books, journals, and articles you read that relate to finance and business and discuss how they have influenced your thinking and practices.

This shows an active engagement with your professional development and a keen interest in industry trends and new ideas.

Incorporating Initiative and Curiosity in Your Interview Strategy:

- **Pre-Interview**: Research the company thoroughly, and identify key financial challenges or successes it has faced. Be ready to discuss how your initiative and curiosity could be beneficial in such contexts.
- **During the Interview:** Seamlessly weave examples of your initiative and curiosity into your responses. ***Use the STAR method (Situation, Task, Action, Result) to structure your answers clearly and effectively.***
- **Post-Interview:** Follow up with a thank you note that reiterates your enthusiasm for the role and reflects on something specific you learned about the company during the interview, reinforcing your ongoing interest and proactive character.

By effectively conveying a positive attitude, high energy, initiative, and curiosity, you position yourself as a priced and dedicated candidate.

One who is fully prepared to contribute significantly to the FP&A team and the organisation.

FP&A Interview Prep Secret Framework

The interview preparation framework we've outlined is precisely designed around practically demonstrating these essential traits that interviewers look for in outstanding FP&A candidates: Positive attitude, Energy, Enthusiasm, Curiosity, Cultural fit, and Initiative.

Each component of the framework—preparation, practice, and execution—is tailored to emphasis these qualities in a practical and impactful manner:

By following this framework, candidates ensure they present themselves as well-rounded professionals. Professionals who not only meet the technical requirements of the FP&A role. But they also embody the personal and interpersonal qualities desired in ideal candidates.

Part 1: Preparation: Laying the Groundwork for Success

Preparation in FP&A interviews is about much more than understanding the role's technical requirements.

It involves a deep dive into the company, its industry, and the people you will be meeting.

Here's how to effectively prepare:

1. Industry Deep Dive:

Stay updated on the latest trends and challenges in the industry, especially those impacting FP&A directly. This might include changes in financial regulations, advancements in technology, or shifts in global economic policies.

Familiarise yourself with key performance indicators and financial metrics specific to the industry. Knowing these can help you speak knowledgeably about how you can impact the company's financial health.

2. Company Deep Dive:

Review the company's annual reports, earnings releases, and any available analyst reports. Understand its revenue streams, profitability, cost structure, and investment activities.

Learn about the company's strategic goals by reviewing its mission statement, vision, core values and recent press releases. This will allow you to align your answers and demonstrate how you can contribute to these objectives.

Assess the company's market position relative to its competitors. This awareness can help you discuss how your role could support the company in maintaining or enhancing its competitive edge.

3. Interviewer Background:

If possible, find out who will interview you and learn about their background. Platforms like LinkedIn can provide insights into their career path, interests, and role within the company.

If you know the interviewer's department and role, think about the challenges they might face and how the position you are applying for can help address these challenges. This preparation helps you tailor your answers and questions during the interview.

4. Questions and Scenarios:

Based on your research, prepare thoughtful questions that demonstrate your deep understanding of the company and its challenges. Questions could range from inquiries about specific financial strategies to how recent market developments might impact the company.

Anticipate scenarios or problems the company might face that relate to FP&A. Think about how you would address these issues, demonstrating proactive thinking and problem-solving skills.

By thoroughly preparing, candidates can demonstrate their capability, fit, and readiness to be the right choice for the role.

FP&A Interview Prep Checklist

Prepare	***Details***	***Your notes and Research links***
Industry Deep dive	*Industry Magazines, websites, Blogs - Understand:* • *Latest Trends* • *Competition* • *Challenges* • *Opportunities*	

	Information Interviews: Conduct informational interviews with Past / present employees from the target company	
Company Deep dive	*Company's Vision*	
	Company's Mission Statement	
	Company's Core Values	
	Review Company Annual Statements	
	Ratio Analysis / Diagnosis / Questions	
	Review Company's Investor Presentations	
Prepare for	***Why do you want to join this, Company?***	
Prepare for	***What are the top products and services of the company?***	
Interviewer Research	***Social media*** ***Common Connections***	
	3 Questions to Ask the Interviewer	
	Anticipate 5 problems the company might face that are related to FP&A and how can you help address them?	
	From the job description list down 3-5 areas where you have experience and build narratives around them.	

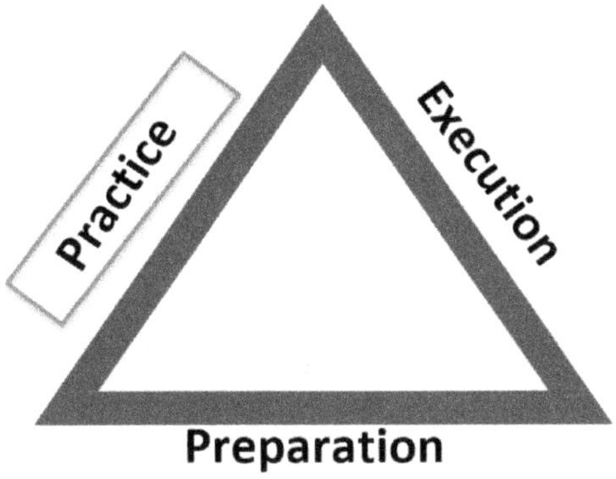

Step 2: Practice and Refining Your Delivery:

Practice is crucial in preparing for an FP&A interview.

Because it helps you internalise your preparation, refine your delivery, and ensure that your presentation during the interview is polished and professional.

Here's how to effectively practice for your FP&A interview:

1. Mock Interviews:

Arrange for mock interviews with a mentor, peer, or coach who can provide a realistic interview experience. Try to replicate the interview environment as closely as possible, including dressing appropriately, setting a formal space, and adhering to a strict time limit.

Request specific feedback on both your content and delivery. **Focus on areas like clarity of communication, body language, and how convincingly you present your solutions and ideas.**

2. Video Record and Review:

Use your smartphone camera to record your responses to common interview questions. Watching yourself can reveal a lot about your body language, eye contact, and the natural flow of your speech. Alternatively, go on a zoom session alone with the camera on and record yourself.

Review your recordings to identify any quirks or repetitive behaviours that could be distracting or detract from your message. **Pay attention to your tone, pace, and clarity to ensure your responses are engaging and assertive.**

3. Practice Common Interview Questions:

Prepare responses to both technical questions specific to FP&A and behavioural questions that explore how you handle situations relevant to the role. Common questions might include "Explain a time when you had to make a quick financial decision without all the necessary data," or "How do you approach creating a financial forecast?" Will cover more of these in the next chapter.

Use the Situation, Task, Action, Result (STAR) method to structure your answers. This method helps keep your responses focused and ensures you cover all parts of your story effectively.

By thoroughly practicing you ensure that you are not just prepared but also poised and ready to present the best version of yourself. Practice is critical in transforming your preparation into effective performance during the actual interview.

Part 3 Execution: Mastering the Interview

The "Execution" phase of the interview is when you put all your preparation and practice into action.

This is your opportunity to demonstrate your qualifications, fit, and readiness to contribute to the FP&A team effectively. Here's how to ensure your execution during the interview is flawless:

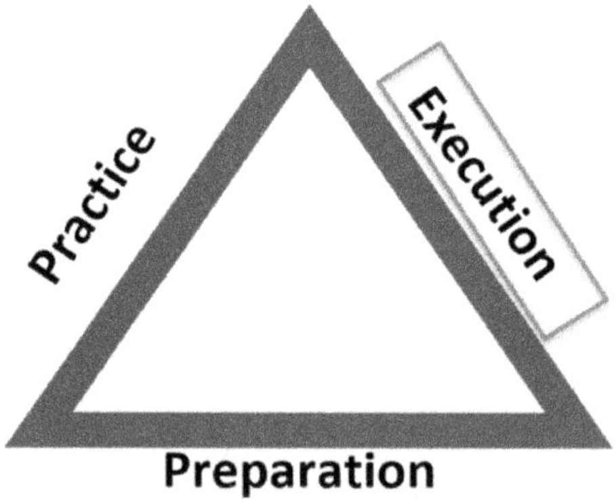

1. **Be on Time:** Punctuality Shows Professionalism. Arrive early for your interview to avoid any last-minute rush and to show your respect for the

interviewer's time. Being on time, or even a bit early, sets a positive tone and demonstrates respect for time and reliability.

Since interviews can be stressful, incorporate relaxation techniques. Techniques such as deep breathing, positive visualisation, or brief meditative pauses can help manage interview anxiety.

2. **Dress Appropriately:** Professional Attire Matters. Dress professionally according to the company's culture. If in doubt, err on the side of formality. Your appearance should convey professionalism and respect for the position you are applying for.

3. **Connect Your Answers to the Company's Needs:** Tailor Your Responses. Focus on how your skills and experiences make you an ideal candidate for the specific role. And how they can address the company's current challenges. Make it clear that you have not only understood the role but also thought deeply about how you can contribute effectively.

4. **Engage the Interviewer with Relevant Questions:** Demonstrate Your Interest and Knowledge from the preparation phase. Ask insightful questions that show you have done your homework about the company and the industry. This not only reaffirms your interest in the position but also your commitment to making a meaningful contribution.

5. **Use Positive, Confident Body Language:** Non-verbal Cues are important. Maintain good eye contact, sit up straight, and use hand gestures moderately to express yourself. Positive body language can convey your confidence and enthusiasm for the position.

6. **Manage Your Responses Well:** Stay Calm and Focused. If you don't know the answer to a question, it's okay to take a moment to think it through. Keeping your composure under pressure demonstrates your ability to handle challenging situations, a valuable trait in FP&A roles.

7. **Close the Interview Strongly:** End on a Positive Note. summarise your key qualifications and reiterate your interest in the role. Thank the interviewer for their time and consider closing with a statement that reinforces why you are a great fit for the position and the company.

8. **Follow-Up:** Send a Thank You Note. Follow up with a personalised thank you email within 24 hours of the interview. Mention specific points discussed during

the interview to show your attentiveness and reinforce how your skills align with the company's goals.

Executing well during the interview involves a blend of preparation, professionalism, and the ability to connect personally with the interviewer.

Sample Thankyou Email

Subject: Thank you for the Interview

Thank you, Mr/Ms Interviewer (XXX),

I very much enjoyed our discussion yesterday and felt that our conversation was very productive.

Moreover, I would like to take this opportunity to convey to you the very positive impression that I gained of Coursera (during the research process for the Interview as well as from our meetings).

In addition to the points that we discussed, I have outlined some perceptions relative to the role's current needs, as well as my capability to make an impact and positive contribution.

Role requirements.	My skills and experience
Edtech Industry Experience	I have 3+ years of experience working with two edtech companies in my immediate previous roles.
Build an FP&A Function from the ground up	I have experience of setting up processes and systems for budgeting, forecasting, management reporting, in my past roles. I am most excited about the opportunity to implement a web-based automation tool for FP&A.
Communicate with the CEO and Senior business leaders	One of my strengths is working with senior leadership delivering presentations and working with business teams on cross-functional projects.
Experience in working with B2B SaaS business and metrics.	I have hands-on experience working with B2B SaaS models and metrics such as Bookings ACV, TCV, ARR, MRR, Retention, Renewal, Churn, CAC, LTV, and more.

What attracts me to this role:

- *Coursera's mission is to help millions of people get access to affordable quality education.*
- *Chance to work closely with you and the CFO.*

I thank you once again for your time and attention, I will look forward to hearing back from you.

Thank you,
Asif Masani

Sample Follow-up Email Template:

Hello Main Interviewer

After meeting with <Intervirewer 2>, <Intervirewer 3> and <Intervirewer 4> last week and our discussions today, I find that my enthusiasm for the position continues to grow.

I also very much appreciate the positive rapport that I feel you and I established during the meetings we have had. Should you or any of your team require additional information regarding my background and achievements, please do not hesitate to contact me at (Mobile) or (email)

I look forward to hearing from you or <HR Contact> soon to discuss what I hope may be a job offer.

In anticipation of that conversation, I thank you once again for your time and attention.

Thank you,
Asif Masani

Sample Job Application Email/ Cover Letter

Dear HR Contact,

I am thrilled to write to you about the FP&A Role. I think I'd be a great fit for this role.

Here are 2 reasons why I would be a perfect fit for this role:

1. *Firstly, I have gone through the job description, and I meet all the requirements.*

2. *Secondly, I have direct experience of 5+ years as an FP&A Manager and FP&A Consultant. In my position at Citi, I have successfully partnered with finance and business leaders on various projects. At*

Pfizer, I am presently working as a consultant with Finance Directors driving business performance.

I think my background and experience will be an asset to your organisation / client organisation.

Attached is my resume. Please let me know if you have any questions.

Thank you,
Asif Masani

Quick Recap of the FP&A Interview Preparation Secrets Framework

1. Understanding What Interviewers Look For

Key Qualities:

- **Attitude and Energy:** Demonstrate a positive and proactive approach.
- **Enthusiasm and Curiosity:** Show a genuine interest in the role and the field of FP&A.
- **Cultural Fit:** Express how your personal values align with the company's culture.
- **Initiative:** Share examples where you have taken the lead on projects or tasks, showcasing your ability to act independently.

2. The FP&A Interview Prep Secret Framework

Part 1: Preparation:

- **Industry Deep Dive:** Research current trends and challenges in the industry.
- **Company Deep Dive:** Understand the company's financial health, competitive position, and strategic goals.
- **Interviewer Background:** Learn about the interviewer's role within the company and their professional background.

Part 2: Practice your Delivery:

- **Mock Interviews:** Conduct mock interviews with peers or mentors to get feedback.
- **Video Record and Review:** Record practice sessions to critique your own performance.
- **Common Questions:** Prepare answers to typical interview questions.

Part 3: Execution:

- **Be on Time:** Ensure punctuality to convey professionalism.
- **Connection to Role:** Relate your answers and discussions back to how you can contribute to the company and support the interviewer/team's goals.
- **Engagement:** Ask insightful questions that demonstrates your deep understanding of the company and the role.
- **Follow-Up:** Send a thank-you note post-interview and follow up appropriately to express your continued interest.

Strategic Interview Framework for Senior FP&A Roles

As you climb the career ladder in FP&A.

Your approach to interviews must evolve to demonstrate not only your technical proficiency and leadership skills. But also, your strategic vision and ability to drive business results.

This framework is designed to structure your interview in a way that maximizes the exchange of information and positions you as the ideal candidate for the role:

1. **Initiate with Open-Ended Questions:** Start by Encouraging Dialogue. Begin the interview by asking the interviewer what they hope to achieve from the conversation. This sets a collaborative tone and shows your interest in aligning with their expectations.

2. Understand Their Perspective:

- Ask About the Company Strategy and Role

- Request the interviewer to outline their current strategy and how the FP&A role fits into it.
- Ask them to describe their ideal candidate and the key challenges of the role.
- Inquire why they think a prospective candidate should consider joining the organisation (which helps you understand the selling points of the role from their perspective)

3. Present Your Case

- Articulate Your Fit and Value: Prepare to give 4-5 compelling reasons why they should hire you, focusing on how your experience and skills directly address the needs and challenges discussed.
- Highlight relevant experiences with specific examples that showcase your ability to perform in similar situations or environments.

4. Engage with Targeted Questions:

Deepen Your Understanding. After presenting your case, ask specific questions about the role, team dynamics, company culture, and future projects. This demonstrates your thorough preparation and genuine interest in the role.

5. Respond to Their Queries:

Provide Thoughtful Answers. Address the interviewer's questions with detailed responses, ensuring to tie back your answers to the skills and qualities they've emphasised as important.

6. Assess Mutual Fit:

Discuss Compatibility. Engage in a conversation about how well your skills, experience, and career goals align with the role and the company's future direction. This mutual assessment helps both sides determine if there is a good fit.

7. Clarify Next Steps:

Agree on the Following Actions. Conclude the interview by discussing the next steps in the process. Ask about the timeline and any additional information they might need from you. This shows your eagerness to move forward and maintains the momentum of your application.

8. Follow-Up

Send a Thank You Note. After the interview, send a personalised thank you email, summarising the key points discussed and reaffirming your interest. This keeps you top of mind and demonstrates professionalism.

This interview framework is designed to ensure that you not only present yourself effectively but also actively engage with the interviewer in a strategic manner.

By asking the right questions and presenting your qualifications aligned with the company's needs, you enhance your chances of success in securing a senior FP&A role.

In the final part of this chapter, we bring to you practical tips from seasoned FP&A professionals, who successfully transitioned from accounting to FP&A roles.

We spoke with more than 20 FP&A professionals. And we asked them the following question "What do you do to prepare for FP&A interviews?'" to understand how they prepared for their interviews:

Let's learn from their experience:

Swati Bagri	***"Although I lacked direct experience in an FMCG company, I spoke extensively with individuals who work in the sector to gain insight. Before my interviews, I researched the company's culture thoroughly to understand how I could fit in. I focused on showcasing the transferable skills I gained during my audit career, which set me apart from other candidates who might have had more industry-specific credentials."*** *Swati highlights the importance of understanding the industry, particularly if it's unfamiliar. She conducted extensive research on the company and spoke with individuals working in the FMCG sector to better understand the cultural and operational dynamics. She*

	also focused on identifying and articulating transferable skills from her auditing background, which helped demonstrate her potential value to FP&A roles.
Jun Nichole	***"Before preparing for an interview, I research the company thoroughly to make sure it's a good fit for me, just as they are assessing my fit for them. It's not just about having the right financial skills; the company's culture and values must align with mine."*** *Jun stressed the importance of researching the company to ensure a good mutual fit, both for the candidate and the company. He noted that interviews are a two-way street where both parties assess compatibility, not just in terms of job skills but also cultural fit and shared values.*
Vivek Sharma	***"When I receive an interview call, my preparation starts with a deep dive into the job description. This helps me understand the expectations and the type of individuals they are looking for. I also research the company's financial health, market position, and my interviewer's professional background to tailor my approach."*** *Vivek systematically prepares by thoroughly analysing the job description and researching the company's financial health, market position, and the profiles of the interviewers. This comprehensive preparation helps him tailor his responses and questions to demonstrate a deep understanding of the company and how he can contribute to its goals.*
Dhawal Parvatikar	***"I focus on understanding the industry, the competitors, and particularly the company's financial standing. I look at their financial statements and annual reports to prepare pointed observations and questions that can demonstrate my thorough preparation and analytical capabilities."*** *Dhawal described a detailed approach to preparation that includes industry analysis, competitor analysis, and*

	financial performance review of the company. He also suggested engaging with product users and reviewing the company's financial statements to discuss specific observations intelligently during the interview.
George Katsimihas	***"For me, understanding why I want the FP&A role is crucial. I believe if you're motivated by more than just a paycheck—like a genuine interest in the business side of finance—it will shine through in the interview. I prepare by immersing myself in the company's financial statements and strategic objectives to discuss how I can contribute meaningfully."*** *George emphasised understanding the real reasons behind pursuing a position in FP&A, suggesting that a genuine interest in the operational and strategic aspects of business finance is crucial. He advised candidates to demonstrate their analytical skills and industry knowledge during interviews to show they are well-prepared and truly interested in the field.*
Ron Monteiro	***"My approach involves three key steps: prepare, practice, and perform. Preparation means doing thorough research on the company's philosophy and the interviewer's background. Practising involves going through mock interviews and refining my delivery. Finally, performing well in the interview includes being punctual, making eye contact, and asking intelligent questions."*** *Ron advocated a three-step approach to interviews: thorough preparation, consistent practice, and confident performance. He suggested researching not just the company's business but also its culture and philosophy to align the interview discussions accordingly. He also emphasised the importance of asking intelligent questions and the ability to discuss strengths and weaknesses articulately.*

Ali Hassan	***"First, I meticulously align my resume with the job description. Then, I study the company's profile, focusing on their mission, vision, and core values, which I mention during the interview to demonstrate alignment. I also review the interviewer's profile to find commonalities that might help build rapport."***

Across all interviews, there was a strong emphasis on the need for thorough preparation that goes beyond the basics.

In this chapter we saw:

- **Key Traits Interviewers Seek in Top Candidates:** Attitude, Enthusiasm, Energy, Initiative and Curiosity
- **The 3-Step Interview Prep Framework:** Prepare, Practice and Execute
- **Practical Tips** on Interview preparation from FP&A experts.

You've prepared well for the interviews, but what questions should you expect? In the next Chapter let's look at 100+ common FP&A interview questions you can expect and prepare for.

Chapter 9

FP&A Interview Questions

This chapter offers a curated list of the most common frequently asked FP&A Interview questions.

Preparing for these questions will help you crack most FP&A interviews.

To keep this book concise and focused on what's most important we have not included sample answers in this book.

Instead, detailed sample responses can be found in a separate bonus PDF accompanying this book or can be downloaded from

https://fpnaprofessionals.teachable.com/

Section 1: Budgeting and Forecasting

1. Can you explain the concept of budgeting in FP&A?
2. What are the main budgeting approaches, and can you briefly explain each?
3. Can you describe the Zero-Based Budgeting (ZBB) method?
4. Differentiate between top down and bottoms up budgeting?
5. What is the difference between budgeting and forecasting?
6. Explain the concept of a cash budget.
7. What is the difference between traditional budgeting and rolling forecasting?
8. How does Activity-Based Budgeting (ABB) differ from traditional budgeting?
9. What are the primary components of a financial forecast?
10. How do you handle uncertainty and risk in forecasting? How do you incorporate risk and uncertainty into financial forecasts?
11. What are the key differences between strategic planning and budgeting?

12. How can a company use forecasting for capacity planning?
13. How does a company incorporate driver-based budgeting into its planning process?
14. In forecasting, how do you distinguish between short-term and long-term predictions?
15. What are the limitations of budgeting, and how can companies overcome them?
16. Explain the concept of a flexible budget?
17. Walk me through the steps you would take to create an annual budget for a company?
18. How do you handle budget variances, and what actions would you take if a variance is unfavourable?
19. What are some common forecasting methods, and when would you use each one?
20. How do you stay up to date on current industry trends and their potential impact on financial planning?

Section 2: Financial Statement Analysis

21. Walk me through the Income Statement / Balance Sheet and Cash Flow Statement?
22. What is the purpose of an income statement?
23. How do you define working capital?
24. Explain the difference between EBITDA and net income?
25. What are the key components of a cash flow statement? Explain the components of a cash flow statement?
26. How do you calculate Return on Investment?
27. Can you name three financial metrics used to evaluate a company's profitability?
28. How do you allocate overhead costs in a manufacturing setting?

29. How does a company's debt-to-equity ratio impact its financial health?

30. What role does ROI play in investment decision-making?

31. Can you provide an example of a company's operating activities in the cash flow statement?

32. What is the difference between depreciation and amortization?

33. How do changes in working capital affect the cash flow statement?

34. Explain the purpose of the balance sheet in financial reporting?

35. Define fixed costs and provide an example?

36. What is the difference between EBITDA and operating income?

37. Can you describe the importance of working capital in financial analysis?

38. Describe a time when you identified a financial trend or a risk?

Section 3: Financial Modelling

39. How do you approach Financial Modelling?

40. What is the purpose of scenario analysis in financial planning?

41. How can you create a dynamic financial model in Excel?

42. Can you explain what a three-statement financial model is and its components?

43. Walk me through the process of building a discounted cash flow (DCF) model?

44. How do you assess the sensitivity of a financial model to changes in key inputs?

45. Can you describe a complex financial model you have built-in Excel? What was the purpose and outcome?

Section 4: Technical Questions on Excel and Tools

46. How would you use Excel to perform a VLOOKUP?

47. Do you have experience with any specific financial software or tools? Which ones?

48. How proficient are you in Excel, and can you demonstrate your skills (e.g., pivot tables, VLOOKUP, macros)?

49. How do you utilise Excel's advanced functions, like INDEX-MATCH or array formulas, in your financial analysis?

50. What is your approach to data analysis when dealing with large datasets in FP&A?

51. How do you ensure data integrity when importing large sets of data into Excel from different sources?

52. Explain how you would use Excel to consolidate and analyse financial data from multiple business units within a company?

53. Explain how you would utilise Excel's data validation features to ensure the reliability of financial data entry?

54. Describe how you would use Excel to create a dynamic dashboard for monthly financial reporting?

55. How do you apply conditional formatting in Excel to highlight key financial indicators?

56. What techniques do you use in Excel to manage and analyse financial forecasts for accuracy?

57. How do you use Excel's power query or power pivot features to manage large financial datasets?

58. Can you describe a time when you used Excel to solve a complex problem in budgeting or forecasting?

59. How do you leverage Excel's scenario manager for sensitivity analysis in financial models?

60. Explain how you would use Excel to track and report on key performance indicators (KPIs) across different departments?

61. What are your strategies for using Excel to streamline financial reporting and reduce manual errors?

62. Can you describe how you would build a break-even analysis model in Excel?

63. Describe how you would use array formulas in Excel to perform complex calculations across multiple data ranges?

64. How do you implement Excel's solver feature to optimize financial decisions?

65. How do you use Excel to optimize financial models for faster processing and analysis?

66. How do you handle version control and collaboration in Excel when working with multiple stakeholders?

67. Describe a method you use in Excel to forecast financial outcomes based on variable inputs.

68. How do you use Excel's advanced charting features to visualise financial trends and data correlations?

69. Can you explain how to use Excel to perform Monte Carlo simulations for risk assessment in financial planning?

70. What are your strategies for ensuring data consistency across multiple Excel spreadsheets within a single financial project?

71. how you would use Excel to calculate weighted averages for financial reporting?

72. How do you integrate Excel with other software tools for comprehensive financial analysis?

73. Can you describe a process for using Excel to manage and reconcile intercompany transactions?

74. How would you utilise Excel's external data connections feature to automatically update financial models with real-time data?

75. Describe how you use Excel's auditing tools, like Trace Precedents and Trace Dependents, to troubleshoot and verify your financial models?

76. How do you apply Excel's What-If Analysis tools, like Data Tables or Goal Seek, in financial forecasting?

77. Describe how you would use Excel to automate the consolidation of quarterly financial statements. How do you utilise Excel's conditional functions (e.g., IF, SUMIF, COUNTIF) to segment and analyse financial data?

78. Explain how you would set up and manage a rolling forecast model in Excel.

79. Can you describe a method for using Excel to track and analyse capital expenditure against the budget?

80. How do you use Excel to perform cross-sectional and time-series financial analysis?

81. Can you describe how to use Excel to integrate and analyse data from non-financial sources to gain deeper business insights?

82. Describe how you would configure Excel to automatically update financial metrics when underlying data changes.

83. Can you discuss how to use Excel for project cost tracking and variance analysis against the original budget?

84. Explain how you would use Excel to develop a predictive model for revenue based on historical sales data.

85. How would you leverage Excel to assess the impact of foreign exchange rate fluctuations on international operations?

86. How would you set up an Excel model to forecast cash flow needs for the next fiscal year?

87. Describe how you would use Excel to automate the generation of recurring financial reports, such as monthly sales and expenses.

88. How do you use Excel's advanced filtering techniques to sift through large datasets for specific financial insights?

89. Can you describe how to use Excel for creating and maintaining a dynamic capital structure model?

90. Explain how you would use Excel to track and manage performance metrics across different business units?

91. Describe a process for using Excel to integrate financial data with operational metrics to provide comprehensive business insights?

92. How do you use Excel to perform time value of money calculations for investment decisions?

93. Can you explain how to create custom Excel functions to streamline repetitive financial analysis tasks?

94. Describe how you would use Excel to conduct ratio analysis and its application in assessing company performance?

95. Explain the process of using Excel to model the financial impact of different business strategies under various economic conditions?

96. How would you leverage Excel's PivotTable features to summarize year-over-year budget variations?

Section 5: Capital Budgeting

97. How do you calculate the net present value (NPV) of a project?

98. Can you explain the differences between internal rate of return (IRR) and net present value (NPV) in the context of capital budgeting?

99. Can you describe a situation where you had to choose between multiplc investment opportunities? How did you make your decision? How do you assess the opportunity cost of choosing one capital project over another?

100. How do you handle uncertainties or assumptions in your capital budgeting models?

101. How do you prioritize capital projects when resources are constrained?

102. Can you explain how sensitivity analysis is used in the capital budgeting process?

103. Describe a method you use to evaluate the residual value of an asset at the end of a project?

104. Explain how you would use the payback period method to assess a capital investment and its limitations?

105. How do you evaluate the impact of inflation on the projected cash flows of a capital ?

106. Can you discuss a time when you had to revise an investment decision based on new financial information or changing market conditions?

Section 6: Management Reporting

107. What is a variance analysis, and why is it important in FP&A?

108. Tell me about a time when you had to deal with a significant variance between budget?

109. How do you prepare management reports that effectively communicate financial performance to non-financial stakeholders?

110. Can you describe the process you follow to investigate and report on budget discrepancies?

111. How do you use variance analysis to inform business decisions and strategic planning?

112. What tools and techniques do you use to enhance the readability and effectiveness of management reports?

113. Can you explain how you would use trend analysis in your management reporting to highlight potential financial issues?

114. How do you tailor financial reports to different audiences within the organisation?

115. How do you incorporate non-financial data into your management reports to provide a more comprehensive view of business performance?

116. Describe a method you use for forecasting and reporting seasonal variances in sales or expenses?

117. Can you explain how automation has impacted the management reporting process in your previous roles?

118. What steps do you take to ensure data consistency and reliability across multiple management reports?

119. Describe a challenge you faced in gathering data for a variance analysis. How did you overcome it?

120. How do you handle discrepancies found during variance analysis before finalising management reports?

121. Explain how you would use variance analysis to assist in cost control measures within the company?

122. Describe your process for updating forecast models based on actual performance data reported in management reports?

123. Can you provide an example of how you have used variance analysis to drive process improvements?

124. What metrics do you consider most critical when conducting a variance analysis for a rapidly growing department or product line?

Soft Skills and Behavioural Questions:

125. How do you communicate financial information to non-finance team members or executives effectively?

126. Describe a challenging project or problem you faced in your previous role and how you resolved it?

127. How do you prioritise and manage multiple tasks and deadlines in FP&A?

128. Can you provide an example of a time when you had to work collaboratively in a cross-functional team?

129. Tell me about a time when you had a disagreement with your manager or colleague. How was the issue resolved?

130. How do you ensure accuracy and efficiency in your work?

131. How will you explain a complex financial concept to someone in the other department with no financial background?

132. Describe a time when you had to make a quick financial decision with incomplete information. What was the situation and the outcome?

133. How do you handle stress and pressure, especially during tight month-end or quarter-end deadlines?

134. Can you share an example of how you have used your financial expertise to influence a business decision?

135. Tell me about a time when you had to learn a new tool or technology to improve your financial analysis. How did you go about it?

136. Describe a situation where you had to go above and beyond to ensure the accuracy of a financial report. What did you do and what was the impact?

137. Tell me about a time when your stakeholder identified a significant error in your report. How did you handle it?

138. Tell me about a time when your analysis led to a significant change in company strategy. What was the situation and the outcome?

139. How have you handled a situation where you had to meet a deadline, but were provided with data that was less reliable than you prefer?

140. Tell me about a time when you successfully implemented a new financial process or system within your organisation. What challenges did you face and how did you overcome them?

141. Tell me about a time when you had to present complex financial information in a simplified manner to a group of stakeholders. How did you ensure they understood?

The questions presented in this chapter are designed to equip you with a solid foundation in FP&A as well as ensure that you are well-prepared for any FP&A interview scenario.

By exploring these common questions, you'll deepen your understanding of key concepts and improve your ability to articulate your expertise effectively.

Remember, thorough preparation is the key to success in achieving your career goals in FP&A.

For a more detailed exploration of each question, refer to the accompanying bonus PDF, which provides sample answers and further insights to enhance your preparation. The bonus PDF can also be accessed at: https://fpnaprofessionals.teachable.com/

After nailing the interview, transitioning smoothly into the role is crucial. In the next section we discuss to overcome these challenges and roadblocks.

Section 4

Approaching The New FP&A Role

Chapter 10

Transitioning Into FP&A - Overcoming Challenges And Roadblocks

Transitioning into FP&A presents a unique set of challenges. These challenges can test the adaptability, patience, and skills of even the most seasoned professionals.

In this chapter, we will talk about the common problems faced as people shift from accounting-related roles into FP&A.

Strategies to overcome roadblock

We interviewed several FP&A professionals who successfully made the transition.

And asked them the following question:

"What were your greatest challenges during the transition to FP&A, and how did you overcome them?"

Here are some key insights. And more importantly, the strategies they used to overcome these obstacles.

1. Mindset Shift

Many professionals, especially those coming from audit or accounting, initially struggled with the shift from a retrospective, compliance-driven approach to a forward-thinking, strategic mindset necessary in FP&A.

"In my experience, the hardest part was adjusting from a retrospective, compliance-driven mindset to a more strategic, forward-thinking approach necessary for FP&A. Initially, in roles like audit, you follow strict guidelines

and checklists. However, in FP&A, it's crucial to understand the business reasons behind the numbers.

I tackled this challenge by researching beyond the surface and understanding the strategic decisions behind the figures, which significantly improved my business acumen."

- Swati Bagri

"Transitioning from audit to FP&A was a significant shift for me. Audit roles are predominantly rules-based, but FP&A requires a more instinctual approach where many skills overlap, but the application differs.

I had to unlearn many routines and learn to think about the impact of my actions on the business, which was initially challenging."

- Ammar Bin Saqib

"My journey into FP&A was marked by the need to develop a keen understanding of not just finance, but also the operational aspects of the business. Coming from an audit background, I was well-versed in looking at the past to ensure compliance and accuracy. However, FP&A demanded a predictive approach where I had to forecast future trends and outcomes.

I addressed this challenge by engaging more deeply with different business units, which allowed me to grasp the operational nuances that drive financial results. This cross-functional interaction was vital in sharpening my analytical skills and enabling me to provide more strategic insights in my FP&A role".

- George Katsimihas

"Initially, transitioning to FP&A was daunting due to the difference in focus between accounting and FP&A. As an accountant, I was deeply entrenched in audit and compliance, focusing on past data. The shift to FP&A required a strategic, forward-thinking approach, which was a significant adjustment.

I overcame this by revisiting financial subjects with a new perspective, focusing more on their practical applications rather than just academic success. This relearning helped me grasp the essential concepts needed for

FP&A and understand the strategic implications of financial decisions rather than just their compliance aspects."

- Shreya Shanbhag

We discuss the FP&A mindset shift in detail in Chapter 2: The FP&A Mindset Shift

2. Understanding the Business and Business Centric approach

Another common challenge is developing an understanding of the business beyond just the financials. This requires knowing why decisions are made within various functions of the company. Sometimes it may not always be financially obvious.

"Transitioning from a compliance-focused audit role to a business-centric FP&A position was tough.

I had to shift from merely identifying problems as an auditor to providing solutions in FP&A. Building a better understanding of the business and engaging with non-finance managers helped me make this shift effectively."

- Dhawal Parvatikar

"Transitioning into FP&A was challenging because it demanded a broad understanding of the business beyond just numbers. As an auditor, I was used to focusing on compliance and historical accuracy, but FP&A required a forward-looking approach and strategic thinking.

To bridge this gap, I actively sought roles in projects that involved financial forecasting and strategic planning. This hands-on experience was crucial in understanding how to apply financial insights to drive business strategy, preparing me to effectively contribute to FP&A discussions and decisions."

- Rohit Daiya

3. Skill Gaps:

Transitioning professionals often need to address gaps in specific skills. Skills such as advanced data analysis and financial modelling. These are more prevalent in FP&A compared to traditional accounting or audit roles.

"Transitioning into FP&A involved significant personal and professional challenges. Initially, obtaining the necessary certifications was financially burdensome, leading me to make personal sacrifices to save money for certification fees. Another major hurdle was the lack of mentorship in the early stages of my career.

Which I overcame by leveraging LinkedIn to connect with industry professionals and eventually find mentors. LinkedIn has been instrumental in my learning process, helping me understand the broader aspects of finance beyond the textbooks, particularly in practical and applicable ways in FP&A roles."

- Ali Hassan

4. Cultural and Process Adaptation:

Adapting to the culture and processes of the FP&A department can be challenging. And particularly when coming from a compliance background with a more rigid structure.

"My transition involved moving from a structured team environment in accounting to handling more independent roles in FP&A. Adapting to managing my tasks alone and interacting with teams across different time zones was challenging.

I improved by prioritising tasks effectively and learning to manage expectations across diverse teams."

- Vivek Sharma

"For me, the transition into FP&A involved adapting to a much faster-paced environment where decisions needed to be made quickly and based on projections rather than historical data. Coming from a strictly regulated accounting background, this required a significant shift in my approach to work.

I tackled this challenge by immersing myself in learning advanced Excel and financial modelling skills, which are essential for the quick analysis required in FP&A. I also started participating in cross-functional meetings

to better understand the various aspects of the business, which helped me contribute more effectively to strategic discussions".

– Arpit Chandak

5. Tools and Technologies:

Learning new tools and technologies specific to FP&A can be a significant hurdle. This includes different financial reporting tools and software that are not typically used in other finance roles.

Coming from audit, one of my main challenges was getting familiar with the different tools used in FP&A. The volume of data in FP&A was overwhelming compared to the audit.

I overcame these challenges by learning how to use and connect various data tools effectively, ensuring I could trust and verify the data I was working with, which is crucial for making informed business decisions.

– Jun Nichole

"In my transition to FP&A, I faced significant challenges adapting to new systems and integrating with various business teams. Initially, the shift from traditional finance roles to the forward-looking demands of FP&A was daunting, particularly with the unfamiliar tools and the retrospective analysis required.

Over time, I took on more responsibilities related to forecasting and strategic planning, such as reforecasting and contributing to the annual operating plans. The learning curve was steep, and expectations have only accelerated over the years, requiring new entrants to deliver within weeks instead of months."

– Abhinav Aggarwal

6. Communication and Presentation Skills:

FP&A roles often require strong communication and presentation skills as professionals need to present complex financial data and forecasts to management and cross-functional teams.

"My biggest hurdle was gaining the confidence to interact effectively with cross-functional teams, including high-level executives. Initially lacking in soft skills and business understanding,

I focused on learning about the business more deeply and improving my communication skills, which were vital in FP&A settings."

- Ron Monteiro

"One of the major hurdles I faced when moving into FP&A was developing effective communication skills to present complex financial data in an understandable way to stakeholders, including those without a financial background. In accounting, the focus was more on accuracy and detail, while FP&A demanded a broader approach to how information is presented and used to make business decisions.

To improve, I took public speaking courses and sought feedback on my presentations from trusted colleagues, which greatly enhanced my ability to convey critical financial insights clearly and effectively."

- Arpit Chandak

To overcome these challenges, the professionals emphasised the importance of continuous learning, seeking mentorship within the FP&A field, engaging in networking to increase visibility, and volunteering for projects that can provide relevant experience.

Additionally, they highlighted the benefit of developing a strategic understanding of the business, which helps in making more informed financial planning decisions.

"During my interviews and initial months in FP&A, the transition was challenging due to the depth of understanding and adaptability required. The expectations in FP&A were distinctly different and more demanding compared to my previous finance roles. Many newcomers, including myself, found the first few months overwhelming, which led some to reconsider their career paths.

However, by focusing on a deep understanding of business and financial dynamics, I improved my performance significantly. Mastering effective

communication and storytelling to articulate complex financial data and insights became crucial for my success in FP&A."

- Gaurav Malik

How to get into FP&A roles without FP&A experience?

Next, let's try to answer the most frequently asked question and one of the biggest challenges getting your first FP&A role.

We asked our expert panel the following question:

How can one get into an FP&A role without having any prior working experience in FP&A?

1. Emphasising Transferable Skills

One of the primary strategies for breaking into FP&A roles is to leverage transferable skills.

Vivek highlights the importance of showcasing analytical and reporting skills from previous roles, especially in areas like accounting or audit. This is crucial because such skills are foundational to FP&A tasks, including financial modelling, data analysis, and strategic decision support. He also advises candidates to tailor their resumes to highlight these competencies, making a clear connection between past experiences and the requirements of FP&A roles.

"*In my journey into FP&A, I found that leveraging transferable skills from accounting was key. Many people struggle to get an interview because their resumes don't highlight the analytical work they've already done.*

My advice is to emphasise any analytical and reporting tasks in your resume. Highlighting these skills can create a link to FP&A roles, making it easier to get those initial interview calls. Additionally, leveraging LinkedIn and your professional network can significantly improve your chances. Sometimes, getting referred by someone within your network can make a big difference."

- Vivek Sharma

2. Flexibility in Role Acceptance

Another key insight is the need for flexibility in accepting roles that may not initially match one's previous level of seniority.

Swati emphasises that candidates might need to step into roles such as senior financial analyst before progressing to manager roles in FP&A. This flexibility allows individuals to enter the field, build relevant skills, and demonstrate their capability in FP&A tasks, which is essential for long-term career growth.

3. Strategic Networking

Networking emerges as a pivotal theme in the discussions. Swati also highlighted its importance, particularly in regions like Dubai, where personal connections can significantly influence career opportunities. This approach is often more effective than relying solely on traditional job applications. As it can bypass initial resume screenings that might filter out candidates without direct FP&A experience.

"Transitioning into FP&A, especially from audit or accounting, often requires a step down in terms of position before you can move up. In Dubai, where I transitioned, networking was crucial. You must understand that if you were a manager or senior manager in audit, you might need to start as a senior financial analyst in FP&A. It's important to be flexible and understand that this step back can set you up for different growth opportunities in FP&A. Also, don't rely solely on online applications; try to network with FP&A managers and other professionals. Internal referrals can dramatically increase your chances of getting an interview."

- Swati Bagri

4. Sector-Specific Expertise

Dhawal discusses the advantages of sector-specific expertise.

He points out that having experience in a relevant sector can be a significant asset when transitioning into FP&A. Dhawal's own experience shows how prior knowledge in a specific industry facilitated his move into FP&A roles that required similar expertise. He advises candidates to highlight this experience prominently on their resumes and during interviews to stand out to potential employers.

5. Long-Term Perspective on Networking

Dhawal also stresses the long-term benefits of networking. He advises maintaining strong professional relationships, not only with peers but also with clients and other industry contacts. These relationships can lead to recommendations and opportunities that may not be accessible through conventional job searches. He shares personal anecdotes where positive interactions with auditors led to job referrals and opportunities in FP&A.

"Getting my first interview call for a non-audit role was challenging but achievable through strategic networking.

Initially, I leveraged my network where I had audited CFOs or senior leaders who then recommended me for interviews. ***Sectoral expertise can also be a big advantage. Highlighting experience in a relevant sector right at the beginning of your resume increases your visibility. Remember, networking is a long-term investment. Maintaining good relationships with everyone in your professional circle, including auditors, can unexpectedly open doors to new opportunities."***

- Dhawal Parvatikar

Other Tips

6. Learn about FP&A.

Start by gaining a solid understanding of the fundamentals of financial statements. Take the time to learn about the specific roles and responsibilities of an FP&A professional. This includes understanding budgeting and forecasting, management reporting, profitability and variance analysis, financial modelling, budgeting, and forecasting, as well as the tools and technologies commonly used in FP&A.

Highly recommend you check FP&A Professional Institute's (FPI's) Books and certifications on FP&A.

7. Consider earning a relevant degree or certification.

A bachelor's degree in finance or accounting can be beneficial for a career in FP&A. Additionally, obtaining a professional certification such as a Chartered Accountancy (CA) or Certified Management Accountant (CMA) can help demonstrate your knowledge and skills to potential employers.

8. Gain experience in finance or a related field.

While you may not have FP&A experience, any experience in finance or a related field such as accounting or business analysis can be beneficial. This experience can help you develop the skills and knowledge necessary for a career in FP&A.

9. Be proactive in your job search.

While you may not have direct FP&A experience, you can still highlight your relevant skills and knowledge in your job search. Look for entry-level positions or internships in finance or FP&A and tailor your resume and cover letter to highlight your relevant skills and experiences.

10. Do pro bono work with NGOs and organisations that need assistance.

Offer to volunteer your time and skills to help them with their financial planning and analysis. This can be a great way to gain practical experience while also making a positive impact in your community.

11. Volunteer for cross-functional projects.

Many organisation have cross-functional teams that work on projects that involve multiple departments. Volunteering for such projects can give you the opportunity to work with financial data and contribute to the financial planning and analysis process.

12. Keep an eye out for internal job openings or internships.

Keep an eye out for internal job openings or internships in FP&A and consider applying if you feel that you are a good fit. These opportunities can provide valuable experience and help you build your resume.

Overall, breaking into FP&A without prior experience will require a combination of education, experience, and networking. With a proactive approach, hard work and dedication, you can position yourself as a strong candidate and increase your chances of success in FP&A.

In this chapter, we explored how to overcome these challenges to successfully navigate a career in FP&A

Key takeaways include:

- Adapting from a retrospective, compliance-focused approach to a more strategic and forward-thinking mindset. This shift is crucial as FP&A

demands a proactive stance on financial management, requiring professionals to forecast and strategise rather than simply review past data.

- Professionals often encounter significant skill gaps in areas such as advanced financial modelling and data analytics. To bridge these gaps, continuous learning and practical experience are vital.

- Engaging with different business units and learning from hands-on projects helps in understanding the nuanced operational and strategic aspects of the business. This not only enhances analytical skills but also aids in making informed decisions that align with the company's goals.

- Adapting to the fast-paced and dynamic culture of FP&A is another hurdle. This adaptation goes beyond technical skills, requiring strong communication skills to effectively present complex financial data in a digestible format for strategic decision-making.

By addressing these roadblocks head-on, aspiring FP&A professionals can set the stage for a rewarding and impactful career.

Challenges aside, in the next chapter let's build a robust skills toolbox for your FP&A journey.

Chapter 11

FP&A Skills Toolbox

In this chapter, we will learn from experienced FP&A professionals on the most important FP&A skill sets.

To do that we engaged with FP&A experts who have successfully transitioned from various finance roles into FP&A. We asked them the below question:

"What essential skills did you find most necessary to develop during your transition to FP&A, and how did you go about acquiring them?"

Their responses provided valuable insights. And, most importantly the strategies they implemented to develop these skills.

Here are the top five skills that came out of the interviews and discussions:

1. Deep Understanding of Accounting Principles

Accounting is the language of business. A strong understanding of accounting principles helps FP&A experts accurately predict financial statements and evaluate the financial effects of business decisions.

According to Jason, understanding the underlying accounting behind every transaction is crucial because FP&A essentially forecasts accounting outcomes. This skill sets the foundation for all other FP&A activities, from budgeting to strategic decision-making.

"A deep understanding of accounting is absolutely essential in FP&A. We're often tasked with forecasting financial statements. Which is all about predicting future financial outcomes based on thorough accounting knowledge. My advice. Take your accounting skills and apply them to structure deals and financial strategies to maximize outcomes, which are critical tasks in FP&A."

- Jason Hershman

This was supported by conversations with Shreya, Ammar, and Brett

"In my journey towards mastering FP&A, I've found that understanding fundamental accounting concepts is crucial because they form the backbone of the work we do in FP&A. It's not about knowing the complex details but rather the foundational elements that help you navigate through financial data more effectively. "

- Ammar Bin Saqib

"Coming from an accounting background, I found that knowing how to construct and deconstruct an income statement and balance sheet was immensely helpful in FP&A. These skills put me ahead of many peers because they form the core of financial analysis and forecasting in FP&A. I'd suggest leveraging any accounting experience as it provides a unique advantage in understanding and managing financial data effectively in FP&A roles."

- Brett Hampson

"In my transition to FP&A, the foundational skill that really transferred from my previous controller experience was my accounting background. Understanding core accounting principles allowed me to grasp finance quickly because the two are closely interlinked."

– Shreya Shanbhag

2. Advanced Excel and Financial Modelling

Excel remains the go-to FP&A tool. Beyond basic spreadsheet skills, FP&A need advanced knowledge in financial modelling.

Ammar Bin Saqib emphasises the daily necessity of Excel, highlighting its universal utility.

"Excel is another tool that's indispensable every day; mastering it has significantly boosted my productivity and ability to analyse complex datasets swiftly".

- Ammar Bin Saqib

Mastery of Excel helps manipulation and analysis of large datasets. It also helps develop predictive models that inform strategic decisions.

Advanced Excel skills, including complex pivot tables, are essential since they directly correlate with effective data handling in FP&A roles.

- Jun Nichole

Financial modelling involves constructing complex models that predict financial performance under various scenarios. This makes it an important skill for Forecasting.

3. Strategic Thinking and Business Acumen

FP&A is not just about crunching numbers. It requires a strategic mindset that can link financial insights to business strategies.

This involves an understanding of the business's operational drivers.

George shared the importance of understanding business operations and the rationale behind financial outcomes.

"In transitioning to FP&A, I realized the critical importance of understanding the business deeply and asking the right questions to grasp not just what is happening, but why.

In my previous roles, such as auditing, I was trained to maintain a level of professional scepticism, which I found invaluable in FP&A. However, instead of just challenging, I learned to engage constructively with colleagues to uncover the underlying business reasons behind the numbers. This shift helped me contribute more effectively to strategic discussions and improve financial forecasts by aligning them more closely with business realities."

– George Katsimihas

Strategic thinking helps FP&A to provide valuable insights that influence business decisions.

4. Effective Communication and Presentation Skills

Communicating complex financial information in a clear and understandable manner to stakeholders who may not have a finance background is an equally important skill.

Jun points out that FP&A often need to explain and justify financial data and projections to non-financial stakeholders.

"For me, developing strong communication skills was of utmost importance in my transition to FP&A. As a finance business partner, you're constantly interacting with various stakeholders, requiring not just clear communication but also the ability to persuade and make compelling arguments based on financial data."

- Jun Nichole

Effective communication helps articulate recommendations in an understandable and compelling manner.

Communication includes writing reports, giving presentations, and having one-on-one discussions with business leaders.

This is essential for building trust and influencing decision-making.

5. Data Analysis and Visualisation Skills

FP&A need to be able to interpret large volumes of data and extract meaningful insights that can influence business decisions.

The ability to transform raw data into insightful visual presentations is key to making predictions and supporting decisions. Advanced data visualisation skills also allow FP&A to present data in a more impactful way.

Shreya discusses the transition from using basic Excel functions to employing more sophisticated data visualisation tools like Power BI and Tableau.

"As I moved deeper into FP&A, I realised the importance of advancing my technical skills. Excel became my daily tool, far beyond basic functionalities. I delved into data analytics, learning how to visualise data through advanced Excel features, pivot charts, and eventually tools like Power BI. This progression was not just about handling data but about telling a story that could influence decision-making and strategy. It's crucial not only to manage numbers but also to present them in an insightful way that supports business decisions."

- Shreya Shanbhag

FP&A professionals who upskill in these five areas are well-prepared to face these challenges.

Here are some more excerpts from the other expert interviews.

"Transitioning from audit to FP&A, I learned the importance of analytical skills and building relationships across the company. Analysing trends and understanding data correlations help in delivering more insightful financial analyses. It's also beneficial to engage with non-finance colleagues to gain broader business perspectives, which are invaluable in FP&A."

- Dhawal Parvatikar

"FP&A requires a mix of hard and soft skills. On the hard skills side, excel and financial modelling are fundamental. On the soft skills side, understanding the business deeply is critical. Invest time in learning digital tools like Excel and SQL, and equally, spend time outside your desk interacting with different business units to understand the operational side, which enriches your financial insights."

- Akshay Phadke

Acquiring these skills is just the beginning. Continuous learning and development are equally important.

"Curiosity and the ability to ask the right questions have been my greatest assets in transitioning to FP&A. It's about using the initial weeks to learn as much as possible about the business from different stakeholders and becoming deeply familiar with the financial and operational drivers. Soft skills, particularly in communication, are also crucial as they help in articulating financial insights effectively."

- Ron Monteiro

Ultimately, the most successful FP&A professionals are those who can combine technical financial skills with strategic insight and excellent communication abilities.

How to develop necessary skills

Here are 6 ways to develop these necessary skills for a successful career in FP&A:

1. Books

Reading is a fundamental way to deepen your understanding of FP&A. Books not only provide theoretical knowledge but also offer insights into practical applications and case studies.

Here are my top 10 FP&A recommended reads:

Sr No	Books	Author	Description
1	All About FP&A	Asif Masani	Understand and master FP&A concepts in an accessible and digestible format. Excellent starting point for those new to the field as well as a good refresher for those with experience
2	Financial Planning & Analysis and Performance Management	Jack Alexander	Essential desk reference for FP&A professionals, offering deep insights into performance management and strategic planning.
3	Financial Forecasting, Analysis, and Modelling:	Michael Samonas	A Framework for Long-Term Forecasting. A Practical approach to enhancing financial statement simulation models, coupled with techniques to bolster a robust planning process.
4	Budgeting Basics and Beyond	Jae K Shim, Joel G Sigel, Allison Shim	This book equips you with an all-in-one resource guaranteed to make the budgeting process easier, less stressful, and more effective.
5	Future Ready: How to Master Business Forecasting	Dr Steve Morlidge and Steve Player	The book answers pivotal questions on forecast accuracy, frequency, content, production methods, reliability and more.
6	Painting with Numbers	Randall Bolten	Guide every professional needs to communicate numerical information seamlessly and effectively.

7	*The Audacious Finance Partner*	*Andrew Codd*	*Reveals The Key Factors and Skills for Business Partnering*
8	*Create value as a Finance Business Partner*	*BoFoged, Anders Liu Lindberg, Henriette Fynsk*	*The book equips finance professionals to transform the finance function into a profit centre*
9	*Effective Data Storytelling*	*Brent Dykes*	*How to Drive Change with Data, Narrative and Visuals*
10	*Storytelling with Data*	*Cole Nussbaumer Knaflic*	*Data Visualization Guide for Business Professionals*

2. Professional Qualifications and Certifications

Let's see what our experts think about professional qualifications and certifications.

"I have hired people from diverse backgrounds such as accounting, business administration, and cost management.

I believe that certifications, while not strictly necessary, do set you apart from other candidates. They showcase a deeper understanding of key concepts, which can be very valuable. Any certification that enhances your ability to analyse data will be beneficial. Practical skills, especially in accounting, are foundational and can significantly aid your finance career."

- Ammar Bin Saqib

"As a CPA myself, I highly recommend this certification. It's not strictly necessary for FP&A roles, but understanding accounting, which is the language of business, accelerates your ability to make sense of numbers and analyse business situations. This foundational knowledge in accounting gives you a head start in the FP&A, making it easier to transition into more strategic roles and enhance your career progression."

- *Jun Nichole*

"I hold an MBA from Cornell University and a FMVA certification from the Corporate Finance Institute.

From my experience, while certifications might not be crucial for performing FP&A roles, they do help in opening doors and getting into roles that offer valuable experiences. They serve as a validation of your skills and knowledge, making it easier to gain trust during job applications.

Most of the practical skills I apply in my role were learned on the job, but certifications certainly helped in getting those opportunities."

- Jason Hershman

"In my efforts to adapt to the FP&A role, I significantly leaned on self-education through resources like the 'Excel Is Fun' YouTube channel. This platform was instrumental in enhancing my Excel skills beyond the basics, which is crucial in FP&A for analysing large datasets and performing complex financial analyses.

I also made it a habit to listen to earnings calls, which, although initially did not seem to pay off, eventually helped me understand the business better. This deeper understanding made my contributions in FP&A more impactful, as I was able to connect my work directly with business outcomes."

- Brett Hampson

"I pursued a SQL Bootcamp and several Power BI courses, which I found particularly beneficial for my career in FP&A. These tools are crucial for handling the large datasets we work with in FP&A. Most of my learning, however, has come from hands-on experience on the job, which has been indispensable."

- Akshay Phadke

"I enhanced my FP&A skills through various certifications, including financial modelling from Udemy and Power BI training.

These certifications were vital as they are particularly relevant to the everyday tasks in FP&A. Understanding concepts like budgeting and forecasting in detail also played a critical role in my professional development."

- Vivek Sharma

"In my experience, advanced Excel and Power BI skills are essential for anyone in FP&A. These tools allow you to handle big data and support decision-making processes effectively. While global certifications are valuable and add

credibility to your resume, it's also important to focus on developing specific skills through targeted courses."

- Md ElRouby

Structured learning through courses and certifications can significantly enhance your FP&A capabilities.

Seek out relevant training and certification programs that offer practical experience and keep abreast of the latest tools and techniques in financial analysis.

For instance, courses and certifications in FP&A topics like Budgeting and Forecasting, Management Reporting, Data Storytelling and Presentations, financial modelling, advanced Excel, and data visualization can enhance your capabilities significantly.

Here are some FP&A course recommendations:

1. **FP&A Masterclass:** Live Group coaching from FP&A Professionals Institute (FPI). The syllabus consists of 4 modules: Budgeting and Forecasting, Management Reporting, Data Storytelling and Presentations, and Finance Business Partnering.

2. **Certified Global FP&A Professional (CGFPA)** from FPI: An in-depth 6-month hybrid certification aimed at enhancing and certifying their skills in FP&A to meet global industry standards.

3. **FP&A Launchpad** from FPI: Self-paced version of the FP&A Masterclass

4. **FP&A Foundations** from FPI: The Starting point you need to build a strong conceptual foundation in FP&A

5. **AFP's Certified Corporate FP&A Professional** - Specifically designed for FP&A practitioners to validate their skills.

6. **FMVA from Corporate Finance Institute.** This course includes 9 Prep Courses, 14 Core Courses and 19 Electives which will help you learn Financial Statement Analysis, modelling, Accounting, Budgeting, Forecasting, Excel, and PowerPoint.

7. **Financial Modelling Certifications from Financial Modelling Institute (FMI)**

8. **Coursera and Udemy** courses on Excel, financial modelling, and data visualisation.

9. **LinkedIn Learning courses**: Excel for FP&A and Driving Business Impact for Finance Professionals.

10. **YouTube**. YouTube is great, especially for learning excels.

    Here are the top 3 YouTube channels for learning Excel, with a wealth of tutorials:

    - Leila Gharani: Her clear and practical approach makes learning Excel accessible for beginners and advanced users alike.

    - Excel Is Fun - Run by Mike Girvin, Excel Is Fun is one of the most popular Excel YouTube channels. It features 3,500+ videos covering a vast array of topics including basic Excel skills, advanced formulas, and data analysis.

    - Chandoo - Known for making Excel fun, Chandoo's channel offers tutorials on a wide range of topics including dashboard creation, financial modelling, and using Excel for project management.

Here is the link to my channel which is the world's first YouTube channel dedicated to FP&A:

https://www.youtube.com/@asifmasani/videos

3. Mentorship and Coaching

Engaging with a mentor who has significant experience in FP&A can provide guidance, career advice, and insights into the industry. Mentorship helps in:

- Understanding the real-world challenges and solutions in FP&A.
- Gaining strategic advice and guidance on career progression.
- Networking within the industry to learn about opportunities and trends.

You can reach out to experienced professionals via platforms such as LinkedIn, Top Mate and many others.

If you would ever like to work with me as your coach. Here is my top mate link: https://topmate.io/asif_masani

4. Professional Workshops and Seminars

Participating in workshops and seminars is great for:

- Networking with other FP&A professionals and learning from their experiences.
- Staying updated with the latest tools, technologies, and strategies.
- Engaging directly with experts and asking questions specific to your challenges.

5. Hands-On Practice

Nothing beats the learning that comes from actual hands-on practice.

Engage in:

- **Real-world projects**: Whether through your current job or through internships, get involved in projects that allow you to apply FP&A concepts.
- **Case studies and business simulations**: These can be accessed through various online platforms and provide practical experience in dealing with financial scenarios.
- **Volunteer for cross-functional teams**: This can provide exposure to different aspects of the business, enhancing your ability to perform integrated financial analysis.
- **Participate in FP&A and Financial Modelling challenges**: For example, the 5 Day Accounting Challenge or the 3 Day Financial Modelling Challenge run by FP&A Professionals Institute (FPI)

Engaging with professional communities, attending workshops, and participating in industry conferences can provide valuable learning opportunities and insights into best practices in FP&A.

From in-depth conversations with seasoned FP&A professionals throughout this chapter, we've explored the various skills required in FP&A,

- We have understood the essential tools every FP&A professional needs in their toolbox. From fundamental accounting principles and advanced Excel skills to strategic thinking, effective communication, and robust data analysis capabilities.

- The importance of continuous learning was emphasized, with a focus on staying abreast of emerging tools like Power BI and SQL, which are becoming increasingly vital in modern FP&A practices.
- By combining these 5 approaches: Reading, courses, certifications, mentorship, and practical experience. You can build a robust skill set that prepares you for advanced roles in FP&A and enhances your career trajectory.

Whether you are starting your journey in FP&A or looking to sharpen your existing skills. This chapter on the FP&A toolbox not only prepares you for the technical demands of today's FP&A roles but also equips you to face future challenges with confidence and expertise.

Equipped with essential skills, In the next chapter lets discuss your strategy for the first 90 days in the new FP&A role.

Chapter 12

Navigating The First 90 Days In An FP&A Role

Early success in your role can greatly impact your long-term effectiveness and career path within the organisation. This is the time to show your ability to adapt, learn, and contribute to the company's strategy and goals.

Now is the time to learn quickly, build relationships with important people, and start using your skills to make a positive impact on the company. Gaining credibility, understanding the company's financial situation, and laying the groundwork for future success.

In this chapter, we've compiled insights from several experts who have successfully transitioned into FP&A roles, sharing their strategies and lessons learned during their crucial first 90 days.

Through detailed interviews, these professionals unveil key takeaways that encompass understanding business dynamics, delivering early wins, building meaningful relationships, and much more. These reflections offer a valuable roadmap for navigating the complexities of a new FP&A position, aiming to equip you with the knowledge and confidence needed for a successful start.

***Disclaimer*:**

The tips and advice provided in this chapter are drawn from the experiences and insights of various professionals who have successfully navigated their first 90 days in an FP&A role. However, it's important to remember that this initial period is often considered a honeymoon phase where it is natural and acceptable to make mistakes. Most colleagues and supervisors understand that you are new to the role and are generally forgiving and supportive as you acclimate to your new responsibilities. Use this time to learn, ask questions, and gradually build your confidence and expertise.

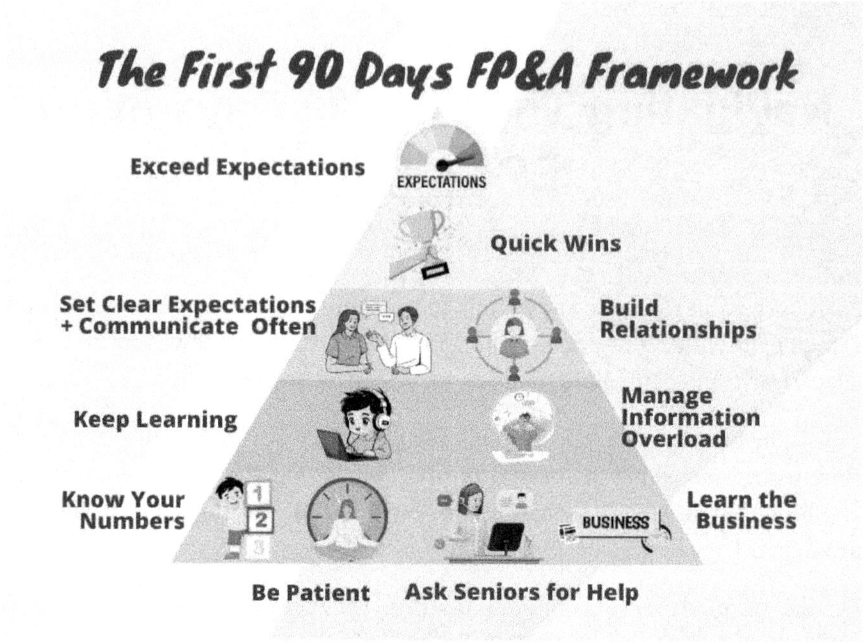

The First 90 Days FP&A Framework

1. Understanding the Business
2. Managing the Information Overload
3. Patience and Learning
4. Listening to managers and exceeding expectations
5. Early Value Delivery
6. Building Relationships
7. Reaching Out to Seniors for Help
8. Setting Clear Expectations and Communicating Often
9. Know Your Numbers, Data Sources and Reports well

1. Understanding the Business

A survey among CFOs revealed that 47% believe newly qualified finance professionals lack business acumen, indicating they can manage numbers but struggle to apply this knowledge to solve business problems.

Interestingly Understanding the business also emerged as the most common theme among the experts we interviewed, highlighting its critical importance in the FP&A role.

This points to the need for FP&A professionals to deeply immerse themselves in the details of their organisation's operations, strategic objectives, and cultural nuances.

The nuanced understanding of the business not only facilitates more informed decision-making but also enhances the ability to communicate effectively with stakeholders across the organisation.

This theme resonates through the insights shared, highlighting that success in the FP&A field is as much about understanding the broader business landscape than just about financial acumen.

Here are some excerpts from the expert Interviews:

Expert Name	**Comments**
Jun Nichole	*"During my first 90 days in an FP&A role, it was crucial to understand the core aspects of the business, its goals, and the culture it promotes"*
Akshay Phadke	*"In the first 30 days, I would focus on understanding the lay of the land and the operational structure, identifying who works where, and the key stakeholders my role requires interaction with"*
Vivek Sharma	*"In the first few days, I recommend anyone new to an FP&A role to really understand the business well. It's crucial to know what drives the company, from its products and revenue sources to the factors that impact its operations. Such knowledge is invaluable when you are tasked with reporting and dealing with top executives. You need to be able to speak their language and understand the business inside out to make a good impression and provide valuable insights"*

Swati Bagri	*"In the first 30 days, it's all about learning the business for me. I recommend meeting as many people as possible across the organisation, from manufacturing to the shop floor, to grasp the business fully. Understanding the process—not just FP&A, but every other relevant process—is vital, though I'm not suggesting learning how to pass an accounting entry. However, sitting with the accounting team to understand the business cycle doesn't hurt. It's about understanding the processes, the business cycle, meeting the team, reviewing past data, and understanding the tools and files currently in use by the FP&A team"*
Arpit Chandak	*"For the first 60 to 90 days, my focus is on understanding the business inside out because FP&A fundamentally supports business decision-making by interpreting numbers."*
Ali Hassan	*It's crucial to understand the day-to-day operations and workflow very well, which means I should listen more and speak less.*
Mohamed ElRouby	*If possible, making market visits in the first 60 days to meet retailers and wholesalers offers valuable business insights. Additionally, discussing strategy with senior executives enriches my understanding of the company's direction"*

Like any skill, business acumen can be developed with practice and focus.

What is Business Acumen?

> *"Business Acumen is defined as keenness and quickness in understanding and dealing with a business situation in a manner that is likely to lead to a good outcome."*

First, it talks about keenness and quickness, in understanding the business situation.

Notice that nowhere is it just sticking to the financial or the understanding of the numbers.

When considering business acumen, it's important to consider the perspective of the business owner and carefully evaluate the situation from all sides, including financial and non-financial aspects, to reach a sensible conclusion.

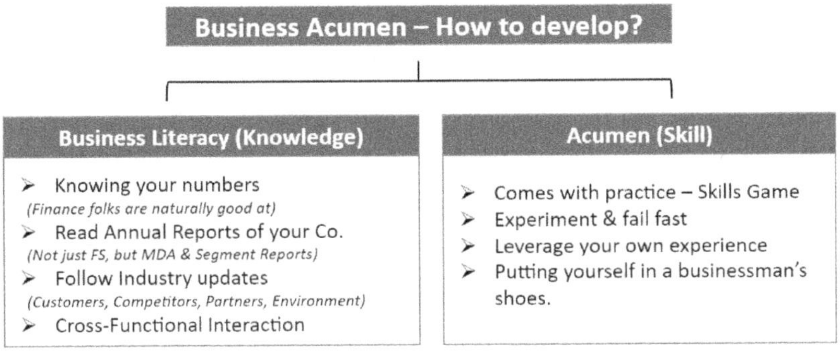

If we must break it into 2 steps. It will be:

1. Business Literacy (The Knowledge)
2. Acumen (The Skill)

1. Business Literacy

Business literacy involves understanding:

- The big picture of the business.
- The interdependence of various functions in the business.
- The business model, revenue model and revenue streams that are to understand how the company is making and making money.
- What are our top 5 products/ services? What are our top 5 costs?
- Which are our best-performing products/ services?
- Which products/ services are not performing well?
- What is the industry we operate in? For Example, is it a monopoly or oligopoly
- Is it Business to Business (B2B) or Business to consumer (B2C)?
- Who are our top 5 competitors?

And more ...

2. Business Acumen

Once you are comfortable with Business Knowledge

Then comes the Acumen part, where it is about your skill and the ability to make judgments and make good decisions for improving business performance.

It's difficult to explain business acumen in words.

It does come from a strong and comprehensive understanding of business, understanding of profitability, and cash flow. It is also not just about the current set of numbers/ historical numbers, but also your ability to foresee some complexities and challenges that are coming.

Here are a few examples:

Example 1

Dhawal Parvatikar shares an insightful example highlighting the challenges of dealing with government clients, particularly those known for delaying payments. He explains how clients from specific departments or ministries, especially in certain geographical areas, have a tendency to not pay on time, labelling them as habitual defaulters.

To address this issue, Dhawal suggested a proactive approach during pricing discussions with business teams.

He recommended increasing the price of products by 2 to 5% to account for the finance costs associated with the delayed payments. This strategy is based on the expectation that these organisations will pay well beyond the usual 60-day credit term, often stretching to 90 or 120 days.

The additional charge is incorporated into the pricing without explicit disclosure to the client, aiming to mitigate the financial impact of late payments.

Dhawal emphasises the importance of finance professionals being able to anticipate these complexities and navigate the commercial intricacies involved.

He also touched upon the risks associated with starting work for a client before a contract is signed, highlighting scenarios where clients might opt for a different service provider after a trial period, leaving the business vulnerable.

This example illustrates the critical role of business acumen and judgment in guiding business teams through commercial challenges, underlining the necessity of strategic pricing and risk management in business dealings with certain types of clients.

How to Develop Business Knowledge (or Business Literacy)?

A. Know Your Numbers

I learned this lesson the hard way.

I remember the day vividly. I had just taken on the role of FP&A manager at a new company. And attending corporate offsite to improve teamwork and alignment during our efforts to regain market share and increase profitability.

During the lunch break, as I stepped into the washroom. There, beside me, was the CEO, a figure I had admired from afar but had never spoken to directly.

As I washed my hands, the CEO, standing next to me, he glanced over and said, "I've been meaning to ask, how are we looking for this quarter's revenue?"

And that new marketing push we started last month, is it making the impact we hoped for on our sales?

I hesitated for a moment, trying to gather the figures that should have been at the forefront.

"Well," I started, trying to muster confidence, "I believe we're tracking... um, we're on target with our projections, and the marketing campaign... it's... um, it's certainly generating buzz."

The CEO raised an eyebrow, a slight smile forming. "I was hoping for numbers, Asif. Buzz is good, but numbers tell the story. Keep them on hand next time, will you?"

"Yes, of course," I stammered, feeling my face flush.

"I'll make sure to have those numbers ready for you shortly."

As we exited, the CEO patted my shoulder lightly.

"No worries, just keep me updated. Knowing our numbers offhand is crucial, especially in these times."

That brief exchange, seemingly inconsequential, was a profound learning moment for me.

As an FP&A Professional, you are expected to know your numbers!

B. **Read Annual Reports: Beyond Financial Statements**

We understand how to read an annual report. We understand the income statement. We understand the balance sheet. We understand the cash flow statement. We are very good at understanding financial ratios like profitability ratios, liquidity ratios and so on.

But to go beyond this. What also need to do is understand the qualitative aspects of the annual report. Most listed companies also include a management discussion and analysis (MDA) section in their annual reports. That's the MDA section where the Board, CEO and senior management discuss opportunities, risks and certain challenges in the company and the industry.

They also talk about:

- What is their vision for their business, and how are they going to tackle these challenges?
- And what do they see in the medium to long term?

So, a lot of things are discussed in the management discussion and analysis section.

It's a good idea to go through that to get an overall understanding of the industry and the business.

Other important reference materials include:

- The CEO's letter to shareholders
- Quarterly Earnings reports

- Investor Presentations.

C. Follow Industry Updates

Establish a routine for staying informed on industry news and integrating this knowledge into your daily conversations.

Keep abreast of industry trends, customer dynamics, competitor strategies, partner ecosystems, and environmental factors that influence the business.

This can be done by subscribing to industry reports and following competitors' social media pages.

You should know who are your top 5 competitors

Who are your top customers? How are they doing? financially?

Example 2

In a discussion with a CFO, Dhawal Parvatikar shared how the executive employs a financial analyst to closely monitor the financial health of their top 50 customers, who collectively contribute to 90% of their business revenue.

To ensure a proactive approach, the CFO subscribes to financial reports from renowned providers like Dun & Bradstreet. This enables the analyst to stay informed about any significant changes in the customers' financial status or potential disruptions due to government or regulatory announcements. Such insights are crucial for the company to anticipate and mitigate risks of lost sales, highlighting the importance of vigilant financial oversight in maintaining business stability. This strategy underscores the necessity of adapting to industry-specific challenges and keeping a keen eye on both customer financial health and competitive dynamics.

Example 3

Dhawal recalls a time when his team was preparing a bid for Facebook, aiming to secure them as a client for an advertising agency retainer. The pricing strategy they adopted was highly competitive, targeting only a 5 to 6% margin, significantly lower than the usual 15 to 20% margins they achieved with other clients. Concerned about the slim margin, Dhawal inquired about the rationale behind such aggressive pricing.

The response he received highlighted a strategic perspective: securing Facebook as a client, despite the lower immediate financial gain, was seen as an invaluable investment. The business team believed that having Facebook on their client roster would not only enhance their credibility but also attract numerous other tech companies seeking advertising services.

This approach emphasises looking beyond immediate financial metrics and considering the broader business impact, showcasing how certain transactions can serve as strategic investments to drive future growth and opportunities.

D. Cross-Functional Interaction

Building relationships across functions to gain diverse perspectives on the business and its operational challenges.

Understanding the business helps in effective cross-functional interactions and builds rapport with business teams, enabling you to get on-the-ground insights. This allows for better management of numbers. Additionally, business acumen, a skill that improves with practice, is crucial. By viewing situations from a business perspective and analysing transactions, you'll gain new insights and enhance your decision-making abilities.

2. Managing the Information Overload

The experience of being overwhelmed with reports and data upon entering a new FP&A role is a challenge. You will be absorbing and making sense of vast amounts of information in a short period, which is a common hurdle for professionals transitioning into new FP&A positions.

Here is a suggestion on how to overcome it.

"One strategy I utilise, drawing from audit experiences, is to create a comprehensive master file when entering new roles. I prepare a file in Excel with important information about the company, including its history, key financial data, stakeholder details, organisational structure, and record storage locations. The master file helps me quickly get to know the company's basics, even though it's not strictly organised. As I learn more about the company over the first few weeks, I continuously update this file, enhancing my understanding of the business, key personnel, and the significance of various reports. This methodical approach enables me to

effectively orient myself within the new environment, ensuring I'm well-prepared to meet the expectations of my role."

- Dhawal Parvatikar

3. Patience and Learning

Rohit's insight on "Patience and Learning" underscores the significance of adopting a measured and open-minded approach when transitioning into a new role, particularly in FP&A.

He stresses the necessity of allowing oneself adequate time to not only grasp the technical aspects of the role but also to understand the broader organisational context and how the role fits within it.

Rohit's advice highlights the journey of adaptation as one that is gradual, emphasising that initial challenges and seemingly simple tasks can evolve into opportunities for deep learning and meaningful contribution. His perspective encourages new entrants to embrace the learning curve with patience, recognising that mastering the role and its responsibilities is a process that unfolds over time, leading to more effective decision-making and strategic insight.

"In my early days transitioning into a new role, I found it immensely helpful to approach it with patience and a willingness to learn. ***Initially, I encountered tasks that seemed rudimentary, like data entry in Excel, which led me to question if I was in the right role.*** *However, I realized the importance of giving myself time to fully understand the profile and responsibilities.* ***I waited for six months to fully understand my role and start taking on the same responsibilities as my seniors. This period of adaptation allowed me to see the value in my role and understand the business better, confirming that I had made the right choice.***

My advice to others in their early stages is to be patient, give yourself time to understand your role fully, and not rush into making any premature decisions about the job's suitability."

– Rohit Daiya

4. Listening to Managers and Exceeding Expectations

Brett's advice on following leadership guidance emphasises the importance of aligning with managerial expectations and directives in the early days of a new role. He suggests that newcomers should focus on executing the tasks assigned by their managers rather than trying to innovate or introduce new ideas immediately. According to Hampson, the key to success in the initial phase is to listen attentively and complete tasks efficiently—slightly faster and better than expected—without overcomplicating the process.

This approach helps in building trust and demonstrating competence without overwhelming oneself with the pressure to innovate from the start. Hampson's guidance encourages new employees to adapt to their new environment by focusing on delivering quality work and following leadership cues closely.

"Your manager will give you the work. In the first 30, 60, and 90 days, you shouldn't be coming up with ideas. Simply, listen to their instructions, follow them, and try to complete the task slightly faster and better than expected. And you're good. Don't try to bring new ideas and crazy thoughts initially. They just want you to do the job, so they can relax a little bit. So, I'd say don't overthink it. Just relax, do the job, work a little bit harder, and you should be more than fine."

-Brett Hampson

5. Early Value Delivery

Jason's advice on "Early Value Delivery" emphasises the critical importance of making an immediate impact within the first few days of starting a new FP&A role.

He suggests that newcomers should focus on delivering something of value, such as a clean, insightful analysis, to demonstrate their effectiveness and contribute positively from the outset.

This approach not only showcases the individual's capability to deliver results quickly but also helps in building credibility and trust within the new organisation.

"In the first few days, preferably within the first few weeks, I want to deliver something valuable, such as a clear, insightful analysis that has an immediate impact.

My success in FP&A roles stems from having a crystal-clear process and setting precise expectations for what I plan to deliver in the first 30, 60, and 90 days, including a comprehensive working model that encompasses all KPIs. It's crucial for me to devise a process and follow it strictly. I communicate this plan right from the interview process and focus on delivering exactly what I've promised. This method has helped me start quickly and has been crucial for my long-term success."

-Jason Hershman

"I focus on quick wins that demonstrate my value to the organisation, working on significant projects while also delivering immediate results through simpler tools or dashboards. This balanced approach showcases my ability to contribute value quickly while engaging in more extensive projects"

- Mohamed ElRouby

6. Building Relationships

Building Relationships is another cornerstone habit suggested by several experts for those embarking on a new FP&A role.

As stressed by the insights of Mohamed ElRouby. He highlights the utmost importance of establishing a solid rapport with colleagues across the organisation right from the onset.

In the first 60 to 90 days, I find it crucial to emphasize building relationships as a top priority when joining a new organisation. Building rapport with people is essential as it lays the foundation for future influence and trust. This is crucial for sharing business insights and knowledge. Before diving into finance operations and deadlines, I priortise getting to know my colleagues and understanding the business deeply. Meeting with individuals across the organisation, from sales to IT and HR, helps me grasp the business's operations comprehensively.

- Mohamed ElRouby

Akshay, Swati and Ali also suggest prioritise building rapport with key stakeholders and understanding operational structures through one-on-one meetings.

"I'd prioritise reaching out, having one-on-one meetings, and coffee chats to express my interest in understanding their work.

It's crucial to get hold of and read as many reports as possible, which are often willingly shared by teams, to help me ask the right questions"

– Akshay Phadke

"In the first 30 days, my priority is to start building healthy relationships and communicate with all departments of the organisation. The healthier relationships I create, the more successful I will be in my targeted role"

– Ali Hassan

"Success in the role significantly depends on building these connections within the first 60 days, leading to a more effective and impactful role in the organisation"

– Swati Bagri

7. Reaching Out to Seniors for Help

Arpit and Vivek advise connecting with experienced seniors to understand their day-to-day activities for a better grasp of the FP&A role.

"When you're transitioning into a new role, utilising the transition time efficiently is vital. I always make it a point to connect with seniors who have experience in FP&A or similar roles. It's essential to understand their day-to-day activities, which provides a clearer picture than any material you could find on Google. Having informal discussions with them helps to grasp what to read, which Excel formulas to familiarise yourself with, and how to use analytical tools like Tableau or Power BI that the company might expect you to work with".

– Arpit Chandak

I advise keeping an open mind and being upfront about your recent transition to a new role. There's a lot to learn from those more experienced in your team, so don't hesitate to ask questions and seek their advice on essential skills to focus on.

Remember, there are no bad questions, and asking plenty can only help you get up to speed faster."

- Vivek Sharma

8. Setting Clear Expectations and Communicating Often

Jun emphasises the importance of setting clear expectations with leaders at the outset, focusing on what is expected on a weekly and monthly basis to make informed decisions.

"My approach involves setting crystal clear expectations with our leaders right from the start, delineating what is anticipated of me on both a weekly and monthly basis. This clarity aids in zeroing in on the data that truly matters for making informed decisions. Establishing these expectations early on is key to streamlining my focus on relevant data and monitoring my progress efficiently. It's important for me to understand the tools and data sources I have access to. I also need to receive any necessary training to perform well in this new situation"

- Jun Nichole

Akshay discusses the importance of becoming more independent after the initial 30 days, stressing the importance of leveraging managerial support to understand expectations and success criteria. He highlights the importance of early feedback and keeping open lines of communication for success and a strong foundation in the role.

"After hitting the 30-day mark, a more directional milestone, I'd start delivering on my responsibilities, becoming more independent. Leveraging my manager to understand the expectations, and success criteria, and ensuring I have the right support is vital. By the 60th day, getting early feedback is crucial to quickly understand if I'm doing well or need to make changes. Keeping open lines of communication with stakeholders, peers, and

my manager is crucial for success. It creates a solid foundation for my role beyond the first 90 days."

- Akshay Phadke

Swati also advises focusing on setting a goal for the next year based on initial understanding, engaging with projects, and building cross-functional collaboration.

"Setting a goal for the next year based on this understanding is also something I'd focus on in the first month. As I progress, engaging with current projects and looking at ways to simplify complex models while building cross-functional collaboration becomes my priority"

– Swati Bagri

9. Know Your Numbers, Data Sources and Reports well

Familiarising oneself with the numbers, data and reports you use is crucial to the FP&A function.

Arpit underscores the necessity of knowing the basic accounting system intimately, as it is the primary source of data for FP&A roles. He stresses the importance of knowing how management currently interprets data, which is essential for meeting and exceeding their expectations.

"Knowing the basic accounting system is also crucial since it's the source of the data you'll be working with. It's important to understand how management currently views data to meet and build on their expectations. During this time, it is important to work closely with your seniors and management. This involves understanding your role, building relationships, and establishing a strong foundation for your future in the company".

- Arpit Chandak

Ali emphasises the significance of studying the company's financial statements over the last five years to gain a comprehensive understanding of its financial health, including profitability, cash flow, expense trends, and capital expenditures. This deep dive into financial analysis is crucial for identifying the reasons behind trends and gaining industry insights. Only with this solid understanding can one effectively predict and forecast the company's future and develop a strategic action plan.

> ***"I believe it's essential to study the company's last 5 years of financial statements to understand what happened in terms of profitability, cash flow, expense trends, and capital expenditure. After that, I dive deep into analysis to grasp the reasons behind these trends and get insights into the industry. Only after this foundation can I move forward to predicting and forecasting the future and crafting an action plan to execute it."***
>
> *- Ali Hassan*

Shreya summarises most of the key points we discussed in this chapter very well.

> ***"Understanding your role within the company, especially in FP&A and finance roles, is vital since these roles are not just vertical; you're not only working with your direct team. You interact with various managers and trainees across the company, managing not just finance but also people, regardless of your position from finance apprentice to CFO.***
>
> ***My advice for the first 90 days revolves around understanding the company, meeting colleagues across different branches, ensuring clear communication about your responsibilities, and being clear in your interactions. These steps are foundational, emphasising that in the initial 90 days, it's more about building understanding and relationships rather than delivering numerous reports."***
>
> *- Shreya Shanbhag*

In conclusion it's vital to recognize the transformative journey a professional undergoes in the initial 90 days of an FP&A role.

This period sets the stage for defining one's career trajectory through strategic planning, keen business insights, and fostering strong, collaborative relationships.

In this chapter, we looked at approaching the first 90days in an FP&A role

Key takeaways include:

1. Understanding the Business
2. Managing the Information Overload
3. Patience and Learning
4. Listening to managers and exceeding expectations
5. Early Value Delivery
6. Building Relationships
7. Reaching Out to Seniors for Help
8. Setting Clear Expectations and Communicating Often
9. Know Your Numbers, Data Sources and Reports well.

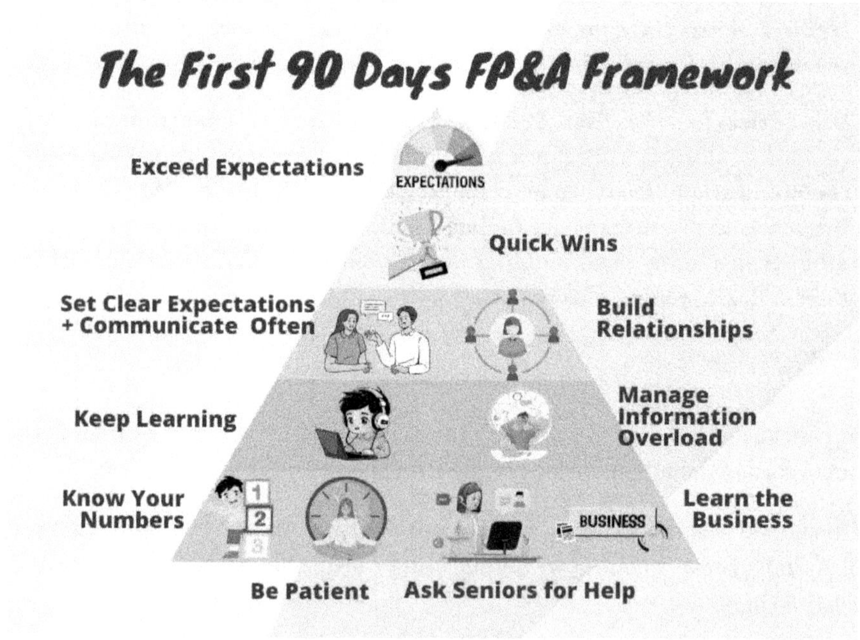

Section 5

Appendix

We are deeply grateful to all the contributors who have generously shared their time, expertise, and insights throughout the creation of this book. Your contributions have enriched the content and provided invaluable perspectives that have shaped the final outcome.

A special thank you to the following individuals for their interviews, which offered profound insights and practical knowledge:

Name	About
Swati Bagri	Swati, a Chartered Accountant, brings over 13 years of rich experience from her work with Fortune 500 companies across India and the EMEA region. Swati started her career in Audit but eventually transitioned to Commercial and Business Partnering roles. She currently heads FP&A for KraftHeinz, MEA region.
Brett Hampson	Brett Hampson is a senior leader in FP&A and is the founder of Forecasting Performance where he teaches best practices about FP&A to startups, SMBs, and finance professionals. Brett started his career in accounting and quickly transitioned into FP&A where he's grown to be the Director of Finance at a Fortune 100 company.
Ali Hassan	Ali is certified CMA and FMVA with experience in various facets of accounting and finance and worked in multiple international organizations. He is currently a finance manager at Bemasa Egypt and board member director at Elrazy hospital.
Jun Nichole Villanueva	Jun is a CPA with experience in various facets of Accounting and Finance and worked in multiple international organizations. He is currently a Senior Accounting Analyst (Financial Reporting) in Sotheby's.
Ammar Bin Saqib	Ammar is an ACA and ACCA, brings a wealth of experience in finance from his tenure in various international organizations. At present, he serves as the Head of Financial Planning and Analytics (FP&A) at Easypaisa.
Ron Monteiro	Ron is a CPA who resides in Canada and has a wealth of experience working in FP&A in companies like Kraft Foods, Campbell's and Kruger Products where he grew from a junior analyst to a senior executive. He currently owns his own training firm KICT Inc. and enjoys speaking and leading training sessions around the world.
Shreya Shanbhag	Shreya is a Chartered Accountant and Chartered global management accountant with over 10 years of experience in

	core finance and FP&A. She is currently based in London, UK as a Group FP&A Manager in Arena Racing Company.
George Katsimihas	George is a CPA, CA in Canada with almost 25 years of wide-ranging experience across strategy, finance and accounting. He is currently a fractional CFO working with founders and executive teams as a trusted finance partner helping them execute their business strategies.
Dhawal Parvatikar	Dhawal is Chartered Accountant and a Certified General Management Professional from IIM- Ahmedabad. His diverse exposure includes CFO & Finance Leadership positions with marquee brands like Bharat Petroleum, Trafigura, Publicis, Omnicom Group & WPP Group. Being the co-founder of FP&A Professionals Institute, and a passionate mentor, he has had a positive impact on the careers of more than 5,000 finance professionals over the last few years.
Akshay Phadke	Akshay is a Chartered Accountant & MBA from Boston University - Questrom School of Business with over 15 years' experience in the areas of FP&A, M&A & Product Management. Having worked with notable brands like Eaton, PWC & Amazon, he is the perfect example of a business focused finance professional. At Amazon, his present role is focused on strategic planning & international expansion.
Mohamed Elrouby	Mohamed is the CFO MEA and Global Finance Lead at Pharmanovia. He is a global finance & strategy leader with more than 20 years of experience in top multinational organizations. including Novartis, J&J, Takeda, Pharmanovia, Allergan and Energizer.
Jason Hershman	Jason is an entrepreneur who spent his entire career building out finance teams at startups. He is usually the first finance hire in and stays all the way through exit. There isn't a thing within the finance function he hasn't seen. Jason's expertise is in FP&A and he has personally used his FP&A skills to grow businesses to phenomenal successes. Currently, Jason runs his own Fractional CFO / Fractional FP&A business where he provides startups with a world-class finance function at a fraction of the cost.
Abhinav Aggarwal	Abhinav is a Chartered Accountant and B.Com. He is co-founder and partner at GA Management Consultants. He has 10 years of

	experience in FP&A, Finance Transformation Projects, ERP Implementations, Data Warehousing, Process Improvement & Business Analytics projects with organizations like Infosys Limited, Sumitomo, Leixir & other global MNCs.
Gaurav Malik	Gaurav is a Chartered Accountant and B.Com. He is co-founder and partner at GA Management Consultants. He has 10 years of experience in FP&A, Budgeting, Profitability Analysis, Financial Modeling, Due Diligence, and Reporting with organizations like EY, Vedanta Limited, Kotak Mahindra Bank Limited & other global MNCs.
Arpit Chandak	Arpit is a Chartered accountant with 9 years of work experience in business finance, FP&A, accounts and operations. He is currently working with FPL Technologies as FP&A Lead. He loves working with numbers and making storyline out of them
Rohit Daiya	Rohit is a Chartered Accountant who explores the world of FP&A. He has worked in various multinational companies in FP&A profile.
Vivek Sharma	Vivek is an ACCA and has 9+ years of experience in FP&A and accounting roles. He is currently working with The Economist as a FP&A analyst and has previously worked with companies like British Telecom, JLL, Ramboll, etc.

We also invite readers to explore the full interviews with these distinguished experts on our YouTube channel. These interviews delve deeper into the topics discussed in the book and provide additional context and examples that are sure to enhance your understanding.

You can find the interviews at the following link:
https://www.youtube.com/@asifmasani

Once again, thank you to all our contributors. Your support and expertise have been instrumental in making this book a comprehensive resource for our readers.

About The Author and Making Of FP&A Professionals Institute (FPI)

Early Days

People who know me are always surprised when they find me on LinkedIn and YouTube, where I write, create articles, and make videos.

Growing up I was quiet and introverted. I was that kid in the class who would always keep his homework up to date to be in the good books of every teacher in the school.

After finishing 10th grade, I felt overwhelmed by everyone's expectations.

It was like carrying a giant mountain of expectations on my back. I felt pressured to choose a career path based on my academic performance.

It was expected that I would take up science and become either an engineer or a doctor.

To meet those expectations, during the break before starting college, I enrolled in science coaching classes. Has anyone else been in a similar situation?

Two weeks into those physics and chemistry classes. I felt like I was a fish out of water. I started feeling frustrated and angry. It became painfully clear that this was not my path. I knew Science was not my thing.

I felt nervous to tell this to my family. But somehow, I gathered courage and walked to my dad's room. He was sitting at his desk with lots of files and papers.

With a hesitant yet determined voice, I gathered the courage and said, "Dad, I can't do this."

He slowly lifted his gaze from the papers. And nodded, showing that he understood how I felt. Then there was silence, like the silence just before the storm.

I thought something big was about to happen.

Then, he leaned back in his chair and asked a very valid question.

"Ok Asif, if not science, what do you want to do?"

I was always fascinated by businesses and wondered how they were run. So, I thought studying commerce might be the best thing for me. My parents, thankfully, were supportive.

College and Chartered Accountancy

With decent grades, I managed to get into the NM College of Commerce in Mumbai. Which was one of the best colleges for commerce at that time (and I believe it still is). After a long time, I felt like stepping onto a stage where I believed I could shine.

Many of my peers were pursuing chartered accountancy. Known as one of the toughest exams in commerce. Everyone made it feel like it was like climbing the tallest mountain in the world. So, I thought, why not give it a try?

Guess what? I loved it! I cleared all my exams in one go.

When I finally added those two letters, 'CA,' after my name, it was an emotional high like no other.

During my CA studies, I also landed an internship at EY (one of the big four CA firms).

Another one of my dreams. I started in audit, and I was initially very excited about it.

But after a few years, I began questioning if this was truly the life I wanted.

Audit to FP&A - A Leap of Faith

Now, this is where things got a bit tricky. I had poured my heart and soul into reaching this point. Everyone around me, including my parents, friends, and colleagues thought I was making a big mistake by even considering a change.

But deep down, I knew I had to follow my passion. I felt like a bright light inside me was showing me the way.

I became obsessed with valuation and investment banking roles. I studied hard, read books, took courses, and appeared in a dozen interviews for those roles.

But fortunately, or unfortunately, luck wasn't on my side. After appearing for half a dozen interviews, I could not land any job in Investment Banking or Valuation. This was the first time I felt I had failed in life.

What I got was an offer for an FP&A role at Citibank.

The funny thing is I didn't even know what FP&A stood for at the time! It was like opening a mystery box without knowing what was inside.

So, I took a leap of faith and joined Citi as an FP&A analyst in 2013. In five years, I climbed from an FP&A analyst to an FP&A manager. In 2019, I took some time off for personal reasons.

The COVID-19 Pandemic

When I decided to re-enter the workforce, it was the 2020 COVID year. This is when the world stood still due to the pandemic. The timing couldn't have been more frustrating.

It felt like the world had pressed the pause button, and I was caught in the middle of this crisis. I gave several interviews, but the job market was tough. Most companies froze their hiring, and some even withdrew offers they had already rolled out due to budget constraints.

Every interview felt like a battle in a war against uncertainty. Despite the frustration and challenges, I continued giving interview after interview. I gave about 8 interviews and failed all 8.

Luckily, I secured a consultant role with Pfizer. It was a glimmer of hope amidst the darkness. It wasn't the permanent job I was looking for, but it provided valuable experience during uncertain times.

After that short stint at Pfizer, I moved to Edtech and worked with companies like Great Learning and Coursera.

LinkedIn and My First Book

In 2021 I began sharing my insights on FP&A on LinkedIn, a topic I was deeply passionate about. Writing a book had always been a dream of mine. After crafting 100+ articles and LinkedIn posts, I realized I had collected enough material to turn this dream into reality. After 9 months of research, and hundreds of hours of writing, "All About FP&A was published in November 2022.

Buy Your Copy Now

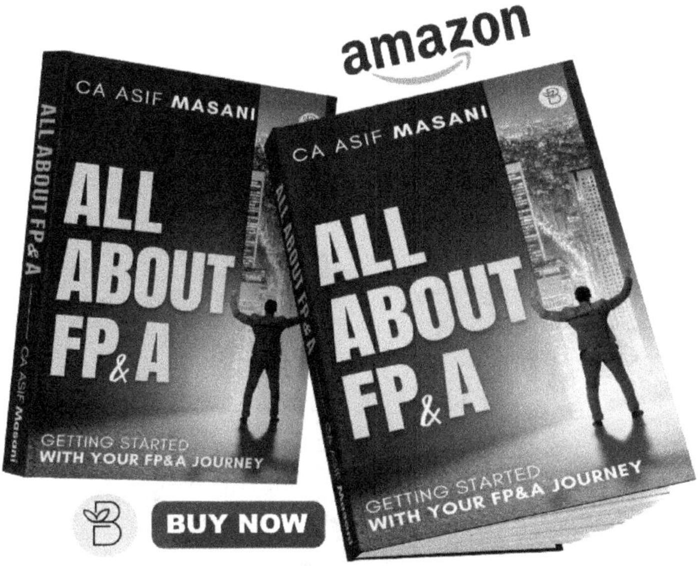

ThePrint

POLITICS GOVERNANCE ECONOMY DEFENCE INDIA GROUND REPORTS OPINION EVENTS VIDEO MORE

Master the fundamentals of FP&A with Beeja House's New Release 'All About FP&A' by Asif Masani

New Delhi (India), December 15 (ANI/ATK): What is FP&A? How can a novice make a career in FP&A? What are the essential dos and don'ts of FP&A? How to achieve your set target on this path of your career? Well, Beeja House's new launch "All About FP&A" by CA Asif Masani is an abecedarian guide to all your questions. The purpose of this book is to give the readers all the important FP&A concepts in an easy-to-understand and digestible format. The readers don't need to have prior knowledge about the subject. Any finance enthusiast, student, or finance professional can reap the benefits of this book.

FP&A Professionals and FP&A Professionals Institute

After publishing "All About FP&A", the response was overwhelming.

I started receiving numerous requests for FP&A training and coaching. This led me to conduct hundreds of free 1:1 coaching calls on Top Mate, where I discovered a significant need for structured training in FP&A. This insight inspired me to develop a comprehensive training program to meet this growing demand.

In 2022, Dhawal (Co-founder FPI) and I launched the first cohort of the FP&A Masterclass, and to date, we have successfully conducted 12 cohorts helping over 350+ students master FP&A skills.

Realizing that not everyone could join live sessions or afford the program, we created a self-paced version called the "FP&A Launchpad."

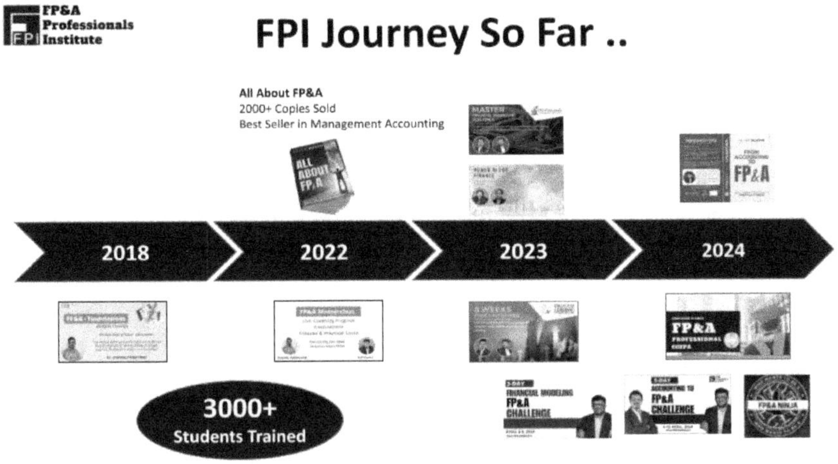

In November 2023, I made a significant decision to quit my job at Coursera and pursue my passion for FP&A education, dedicating myself to writing and building training programs for FP&A and Finance professionals.

Most recently in May 2024, we launched our first cohort of CGFPA (Certified Global FP&A Professional) which is an in-depth 6-month FP&A Certification Program.

Handles

Instagram: /asif_masani/
Facebook: /asif.masani/
LinkedIn: /in/asifmasani/
Youtube: asifmasani
X:/asif_masani

Glossary

Accruals: *Money that has been earned or incurred but not yet recorded in financial statements.*

Amortization: *The process of gradually paying off a debt over a set period, or the gradual reduction in value of an intangible asset.*

Assets: *Resources owned by a company that have economic value and can provide future benefits.*

Audit: *An official inspection of an organization's accounts, typically by an independent body.*

Balance Sheet: *A financial statement that summarizes a company's assets, liabilities, and equity at a specific point in time.*

Benchmarking: *Comparing a company's performance metrics to industry standards or best practices.*

Break Even Analysis: *A calculation to determine the level of sales needed to cover total costs, with neither profit nor loss.*

Budgeting: *The process of creating a plan to generate revenues and spend money, allocating resources for various expenses and investments.*

Capital Expenditure (Capex): *Money spent by a business to acquire or maintain fixed assets such as buildings, machinery, and equipment.*

Cash Flow Statement: *A financial statement that shows the inflows and outflows of cash within a company over a specific period.*

Cost of Goods Sold (COGS): *The direct costs attributable to the production of the goods sold by a company.*

Contingent Liabilities: *Potential future financial obligations that depend on the outcome of uncertain events, such as pending lawsuits.*

Current Liabilities: *Obligations that are due to be settled within one year.*

Deferred Revenue: *Money received for goods or services that have not yet been delivered or performed.*

Depreciation: *The reduction in value of a tangible asset over time due to wear and tear or obsolescence.*

Debt Financing: *Raising funds for company operations or expansion by borrowing money.*

Discounted Cash Flow (DCF): *A valuation method used to estimate the value of an investment based on its expected future cash flows.*

EBITDA: *Earnings Before Interest, Taxes, Depreciation, and Amortization; a measure of a company's overall financial performance.*

Earnings Per Share (EPS): *A company's profit divided by the outstanding shares of its common stock.*

Equity: *The value of an ownership interest in the company, calculated as total assets minus total liabilities.*

Financial Modelling: *Creating a summary of a company's expenses and earnings, typically in the form of a spreadsheet, to predict the impact of future events or decisions.*

Fixed Assets: *Long-term tangible assets such as property, plant, and equipment used in the operations of a business.*

Forecasting: *The process of making predictions of the future based on past and present data and analysis of trends.*

Forex Management: *Managing the risk of currency exchange rate fluctuations.*

GAAP (Generally Accepted Accounting Principles): *Standard accounting rules and guidelines used in the preparation of financial statements.*

Goodwill: *An intangible asset that arises when one company acquires another for a price higher than the fair market value of its net assets.*

Gross Margin: *The difference between revenue and the cost of goods sold, expressed as a percentage of revenue.*

Hedging: *Using financial instruments to reduce or eliminate the risk of adverse price movements in an asset.*

Income Statement: *A financial statement that shows a company's revenue and expenses over a specific period, typically a fiscal quarter or year.*

Internal Rate of Return (IRR): *The discount rate that makes the net present value (NPV) of an investment zero.*

Leverage: *The use of borrowed money to increase the potential return of an investment.*

Liabilities: *Debts or obligations that a company owes to others.*

Liquidity: *The ease with which an asset can be converted into cash without affecting its market price.*

Market Capitalization: *The total market value of a company's outstanding shares of stock.*

Net Income: *The total profit of a company after all expenses have been deducted from revenues.*

Net Present Value (NPV): *The difference between the present value of cash inflows and outflows over a period of time.*

Operating Expenses (OPEX): *The costs required for the day-to-day functioning of a business.*

Profit and Loss Statement (P&L): *A financial statement that summarizes revenues, costs, and expenses during a specific period.*

Profit Margin: *A measure of profitability calculated as net income divided by revenue, expressed as a percentage.*

Phasing: *Adjusting the timing of expenses or revenues to better align with financial reporting periods.*

Project Finance: *The financing of long-term infrastructure and industrial projects based on the projected cash flows of the project rather than the balance sheets of its sponsors.*

Reconciliation: *The process of ensuring that two sets of records (usually the balances of two accounts) are in agreement.*

Return on Investment (ROI): *A measure used to evaluate the efficiency or profitability of an investment.*

Retained Earnings: *The accumulated net income that a company retains rather than distributing it to shareholders as dividends.*

Revenue Recognition: *The accounting principle dictating the specific conditions under which revenue is recognized or accounted for.*

Risk Management: *The process of identifying, assessing, and controlling threats to an organization's capital and earnings.*

Sarbanes-Oxley Act (SOX): *A law passed to protect investors from the possibility of fraudulent accounting activities by corporations.*

Securities and Exchange Commission (SEC): *A U.S. government agency responsible for regulating the securities markets and protecting investors.*

Shareholder Equity: *The residual interest in the assets of the entity after deducting liabilities, essentially the net assets of a company.*

Supply Chain Finance: *Financial practices that optimize working capital and liquidity within the supply chain by enabling faster payments to suppliers.*

Treasury: *The department responsible for managing an organization's financial assets, including managing cash flow, investments, and financial risk.*

Variable Costs: *Costs that vary directly with the level of production or sales.*

Working Capital: *The difference between a company's current assets and current liabilities, indicating the liquidity available for day-to-day operations.*

References

- *Excerpts from the FP&A Masterclass Curriculum by Asif Masani and Dhawal Parvatikar at FP&A Professionals Institute (FPI)*
- *All About FP&A Book by Asif Masani*
- *FP&A Foundations program by Dhawal Parvatikar.*
- *Right skilling FP&A Framework by Asif Masani published by AFP (Association for Finance Professionals)*
- *Transcripts of online live interviews with experts including Abhinav Aggarwal, Akshay Phadke, Dhawal Parvatikar, Swati Bagri, Brett Hampson, Jason Hershman, Mohamed ELRouby, Rohit Daiya, Arpit Chandak, Shreya Shanbhag, Vivek Sharma, Ron Monteiro, Gaurav Malik, George Katsimihas, Ali Hassan, Ammar Bin Saqib and Jun Nichole Villanueva*
- *The Five Why Technique by Ohno, Taiichi.* Toyota Production System: Beyond Large-Scale Production. *Productivity Press, 1988.*
- *Interview Prep Secrets Framework, inspired by discussions with Ron Monteiro and his 3P Interview Framework, as featured in the All About FP&A Podcast with Asif Masani*
- *Excerpts from online Finance Business Partner Training course by Late Andy Shambrook*
- *ChatGPT, a language model developed by OpenAI as a brainstorming partner to generate ideas for the book outline.*

FP&A Professional Institute (FPI) Programs and Books

Can be accessed at: https://fpnaprofessionals.teachable.com/

1. **FP&A Masterclass (*Live and Interactive*)**

Direct access to expert instructors with 2 decades of combined FFP&A experience in 5 different industries. Live group coaching along with practical cases, examples and interactive group activities.

2. **FP&A Launchpad (Self-paced)**

Self-paced version of FP&A Masterclass excluding Live discussions, Q&A, Group activities and experiential learning. Same syllabus as FP&A Masterclass.

3. **FP&A Foundations (Self-Paced)**

Everything you need to build a strong conceptual foundation in FP&A.

Available in Udemy and FPI

4. **Financial Modelling for FP&A (*Live and Interactive*)**

Learn the fundamentals of Financial Modelling and build a strong foundation for financial analysis, Budgeting and Forecasting.

5. **CGFPA: Certified Global FP&A Professional (Live 6-month Certification)**

A six month and 100+ hours in depth certification. It is a designation for finance professionals aimed at certifying their skills in FP&A to meet global industry standards.

6. **All About FP&A (Book)**

The purpose of this book is to give you all the important FP&A concepts. And to do that in an easy-to-understand and digestible format. This book is for you if you are:

- **A beginner in finance** *and want to* **explore FP&A** *as a career option.*

- **A new FP&A professional.** *FP&A is not a part of the curriculum in college and professional finance degrees. Freshers getting into this profile don't have a lot of background when they start. Mostly they learn these skills on the job. This book will help you* **bridge the gap** *faster.*

- **A mid-career professional.** *If you want to* **transition** *from other profiles like accounting and audit into FP&A, but don't know where to start, this could be a great starting point.*

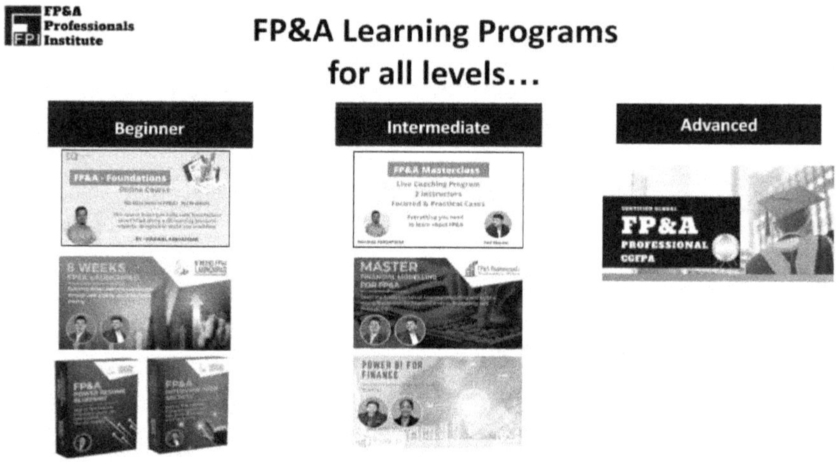

Printed in the USA
CPSIA information can be obtained
at www.ICGtesting.com
LVHW011810160824
788486LV00002B/255

9 788119 682096